D1003247

Complete Guide to Special Teams

American Football Coaches Association

Edited by
Bill Mallory and Don Nehlen

Human Kinetics

Library of Congress Cataloging-in-Publication Data

Complete guide to special teams / American Football Coaches Association; edited by Bill Mallory and Don Nehlen.
    p. cm.
  Includes index.
  ISBN 0-7360-5291-7 (soft cover)
  1. Special teams (Football) 2. Football--Coaching. I. Mallory, Bill. II. Nehlen, Don. III. American Football Coaches Association.
  GV951.85.C66 2005
  796.332'07'7--dc22

2004020518

ISBN: 0-7360-5291-7

Copyright © 2005 by Human Kinetics Publishers, Inc.

All rights reserved. Except for use in a review, the reproduction or utilization of this work in any form or by any electronic, mechanical, or other means, now known or hereafter invented, including xerography, photocopying, and recording, and in any information storage and retrieval system, is forbidden without the written permission of the publisher.

Developmental Editor: Cynthia McEntire; **Assistant Editor:** Scott Hawkins; **Copyeditor:** Alisha Jeddeloh; **Proofreader:** Sarah Wiseman; **Indexer:** Dan Connolly; **Permission Manager:** Toni Harte; **Graphic Designer:** Nancy Rasmus; **Graphic Artist:** Sandra Meier; **Photo Manager:** Dan Wendt; **Cover Designer:** Keith Blomberg; **Photographer (cover):** courtesy Virginia Tech/Dave Knachel; **Art Manager:** Kareema McLendon; **Illustrator:** Argosy; **Printer:** United Graphics

Human Kinetics books are available at special discounts for bulk purchase. Special editions or book excerpts can also be created to specification. For details, contact the Special Sales Manager at Human Kinetics.

Printed in the United States of America

10 9 8 7 6 5 4 3 2 1

Human Kinetics
Web site: www.HumanKinetics.com

United States: Human Kinetics
P.O. Box 5076
Champaign, IL 61825-5076
800-747-4457
e-mail: humank@hkusa.com

Canada: Human Kinetics
475 Devonshire Road Unit 100
Windsor, ON N8Y 2L5
800-465-7301 (in Canada only)
e-mail: orders@hkcanada.com

Europe: Human Kinetics
107 Bradford Road
Stanningley
Leeds LS28 6AT, United Kingdom
+44 (0) 113 255 5665
e-mail: hk@hkeurope.com

Australia: Human Kinetics
57A Price Avenue
Lower Mitcham, South Australia 5062
08 8277 1555
e-mail: liaw@hkaustralia.com

New Zealand: Human Kinetics
Division of Sports Distributors NZ Ltd.
P.O. Box 300 226 Albany
North Shore City
Auckland
0064 9 448 1207
e-mail: blairc@hknewz.com

Complete Guide to Special Teams

American Football Coaches Association

CONTENTS

PART I **TACTICS**

PART II **TECHNIQUES**

FOREWORD

FRANK BEAMER
Virginia Tech

It always made perfect sense to me that the quickest way to win a football game was with special teams. Every special teams play involves big yardage, momentum, or scoring (sometimes all three) in the same play. If a team punts well against you, you lose more than 40 yards down the field. But if you can block that punt, they give up 40 yards plus you have the chance to pick up the ball and score. You get points from the play, and certainly momentum shifts to your side. If a team attempts a field goal and you block it and score on the block, that's a 10 point difference—the 3 points they didn't score, the 6 points you scored on the touchdown, and the 1 extra point. A punt return for a touchdown means your offense doesn't have to try to pick up yards plus you get the points and momentum. No doubt, effective special teams play is the quickest way to put points on the board and win a football game.

The coaches and players I've been around in my career have always been serious about the kicking game. As a player, I blocked for Frank Loria, who was a great punt returner. His returns affected so many games. I played and coached under Coach Jerry Claiborne. Coach Claiborne emphasized every small detail in the kicking game. I then coached at The Citadel under Bobby Ross, who later became the special teams coach for the Kansas City Chiefs, a job he recommended me for and I later interviewed for while a coach at Murray State. Coach Ross had a background in special teams. Nothing changed when I worked with Mike Gottfried. We spent many hours talking and coaching special teams. Everyone I have ever been around in my career emphasized special teams, so it was natural for me to do the same.

We have had great success in special teams here at Virginia Tech. While playing on Tech's special teams, 24 different players have scored touchdowns. In 1998, the Hokies ranked eighth nationally in punting, and in 1999 we were ninth nationally in kickoff returns. During the 2000 season, Tech led the nation in punt returns. During the 2003 season, we ranked fifth in punt returns as a team, while DeAngelo Hall finished fifth among individuals in punt returns and Mike Imoh finished third nationally in kickoff returns. Tech's tradition for blocking kicks has produced 101 blocks in 201 games in the past 17 years. The Hokies have blocked 52 punts (15 for touchdowns), 28 field goals, and 21 extra points. During the 1990s, Tech blocked more kicks than any other Division IA team.

This book will help you better coach special teams. It provides tactical and technical information that will benefit your squad. It will teach you how to give proper instruction to your players, which in turn will lead to excellent execution and positive results. I recommend this book very strongly. I believe in the material it contains. Let it help you win football games. After all, special teams play is the quickest way to win football games.

INTRODUCTION

Relegated in the past to a third priority after offense and defense, special teams play has become a higher priority for many coaches in recent years. Not only is it football's version of the transition game, it also accounts for many of the points scored by and against a team each season.

Strong special teams units bolster a team's offensive and defensive attacks by scoring, denying a score, or gaining advantageous field position. A kickoff team that pins an opponent back deep on its own end of the field not only forces the offense to move the ball further for a field goal or touchdown, it also allows the defense to pressure the opposition more aggressively. Similarly, a punt return team that consistently brings the ball back upfield increases the chances for the offensive unit to score.

More dramatic and well-publicized plays on special teams in big games through the years have only heightened the focus on this dimension of the sport. Easiest to recall are the plays that went awry. Who could forget Buffalo Bills kicker Scott Norwood's errant attempt in the closing seconds of Super Bowl XXV, which allowed the New York Giants to win the title game 20 to 19? The misfortunes of Florida State University field goal kickers versus the University of Miami in critical games in 1991, 1992, and 2000 inspired a phrase that is now part of the sport's vernacular—the dreaded "wide right."

Often lost in such memories is the role the opponent played to prompt the embarrassing, and sometimes fatal, special teams play. Labeled by many as the most comical play in Super Bowl history, who could forget the blocked field goal attempt that Miami Dolphins field goal kicker Garo Yepremian scooped up and then turned over to Washington Redskin Mike Bass in the closing minutes of Super Bowl VII? The undefeated championship Dolphins, considered by many football historians as one of the best teams in the history of the game, were hardly known for such errors. Yet Redskins coach George Allen, one of the all-time leading proponents of special teams play, demonstrated how placing a great emphasis on the kicking game could pay off in a big game against a superior team.

Even without such memorable examples, the significance of special teams play should be clear to anyone who's played or coached the game. Check the stats after each weekend's games and see how many otherwise relatively close contests are determined by the kicking game. Special teams play and turnovers are often the decisive factors when teams are evenly matched.

The challenge is that the tactical and technical elements of special teams play are so many and so detailed that few fully understand them. Still fewer are capable of teaching them.

Complete Guide to Special Teams is both an invaluable resource for understanding the skills and strategies of the kicking game and a tremendous instructional tool. Written by our own special team of coaches, each chapter is crafted by an expert in a particular phase of special teams play.

You'll not find more authoritative, detailed, and comprehensive coverage of special teams play in any other book. And to guarantee that the respective parts of the book addressed every key topic, two highly accomplished former coaches, Bill Mallory and Don Nehlen, evaluated the relevance, accuracy, and consistency of all the chapters.

Careful thought was given to each element of this work so that it fulfilled the promise of its title. Two guiding principles dictated the selection of each topic: its significance to special teams performance, especially at the high-school and college levels; and the importance of teaching the topic to players and units who are assigned special team responsibilities.

To add to the on-field application of the material, *Complete Guide to Special Teams* contains many drills that are especially effective for learning and mastering special teams techniques and tactics. Each part ends with a chapter that helps put together all the pieces from the preceding chapters in that part.

Reading this book and even applying the knowledge it provides won't prevent every conceivable kicking game miscue. As pointed out before, even special teams players and teams coached by greats like Miami's Don Shula, Buffalo's Marv Levy, and Florida State's Bobby Bowden are susceptible to the occasional lapse.

However, with the proper emphasis on special teams play and effective teaching of tactical and technical facets of the kicking game, you can ensure better and more consistent performance throughout each season. And that's likely to mean the difference between winning or losing two to three contests each year.

The key punt block, field goal, or kickoff return doesn't happen by chance. Use *Complete Guide to Special Teams* to ensure your teams are fully prepared to win in every phase of the game.

KEY TO DIAGRAMS

✕	Coverage player/defender
◯	Player on kicking team
◖	Side of block
●	Center/snapper
⊢	Block
➔	Run
●—	Run and stop
--▶	Alternate route
GL	Goal line
🏈	Football
L1, L2, etc.	Left players
R1, R2, etc.	Right players
△	Cone
▭	Dummies

POSITION ABBREVIATIONS

C	Center, corner
E	End
FB	Fullback
FS	Free safety
G	Guard
H	Holder
K	Kicker
LB	Linebacker
LB, RB	Left, right backer
LG, RG	Left, right guard
LGN, RGN	Left, right gunner
LT, RT	Left, right tackle
LW, RW	Left, right wing
M	Middle linebacker
N	Nose tackle
P	Punter
PK	Place kicker
PP	Personal protector
PR	Punt returner
QB	Quarterback
R	Returner
RB	Running back
RE	Rush end
S	Strong-side linebacker, safety
SC	Scoop corner
SPC	Sprint corner
SS	Strong safety
T	Tackle
TB	Tailback
TE, Y, U	Tight end
W	Weak-side linebacker
WB	Whip backer
WR, Z, X	Wide receiver

PART I

TACTICS

BILL MALLORY

The kicking game is an important part of football, but it often does not get the emphasis that offense and defense receive. One out of every five plays in a football game is a special teams play. Often the kicking game determines whether the game is won or lost.

It is frustrating when a breakdown in the kicking game contributes to a loss. I felt this frustration while coaching at Indiana in 1986 in a game against our archrival, Purdue. The score was 17 to 15 in favor of Purdue with less than one minute remaining in the game. We moved the ball to Purdue's 18-yard line and faced a fourth down with 4 yards to go. We lined up for the winning field goal with the best kicker in the Big 10, Pete Stoyanovich. Pete was not the cause of the breakdown, however. The breakdown occurred in our protection. We spent a lot of practice time on extra point and field protection, but we did not protect properly on this play and we lost the game. It is easy to make excuses but the bottom line is that it is the responsibility of the head coach and assistant coaches to see that this does not happen.

You can never give the kicking game enough practice time. The most important part of kicking game practice is working on pressure situations. Putting your players in a situation like the one in the Purdue game will prepare them to face the challenge when it happens in a game.

Complete Guide to Special Teams is divided into two sections: tactics and techniques. In the tactics section, each contributor has written about a phase of the kicking game, explaining different systems, strategies, and methods for teaching that phase.

Robin Ross of the University of Oregon writes about the punt, which in my opinion is the most important phase of the kicking game. Coach Ross talks about personnel selection, the punt team checklist, and protection. He also illustrates blocking fronts. After reviewing punt coverage, Coach Ross describes Oregon's favorite fake runs, passes, and drills.

Greg McMahon, special teams coach at the University of Illinois, covers kickoffs. Coach McMahon presents his team's philosophy, coverage principles, and huddles and alignments. He discusses the middle wedge, middle kick responsibilities, the directional kick, the squib kick, the kick after a safety, and the onside kick. He includes a sample practice schedule and several drills.

John Harbaugh, the special teams coach for the Philadelphia Eagles, discusses punt returns. In his chapter, Coach Harbaugh addresses punt returners and the punt return team. He covers philosophy, technique, responsibilities, and drills.

University of Alabama coach Dave Ungerer writes about kickoff returns. In his chapter, Coach Ungerer presents Alabama's philosophy, the fundamentals of the kickoff return, coaching points to stress, and different returns.

University of Iowa coaches Lester Erb and Ron Aiken cover extra points and field goals. Coach Erb discusses extra point and field goal protection, including huddles and alignments, personnel selection, and blocking assignments and coverages. He also covers coaching responsibilities, practice schedules, and special situations. Coach Aiken covers extra point and field goal blocking, ways to teach and implement a plan, right and left blocks, jump blocks, field goal safes, and alignments versus gate formations.

Urban Meyer, head football coach at the University of Utah, writes about two-point conversions. Coach Meyer discusses Utah's plan to win, the red-zone approach, his philosophy regarding two-point conversions, and the two-point conversion package.

Coach Bud Foster of Virginia Tech discusses punt and kick blocks, including personnel selection, drills to improve and reinforce skills, and punt and kick blocking techniques. Coach Foster's discussion also includes rushes and blocks against the punt, extra point, and field goal. Finally, he explains the practice format used at Virginia Tech.

Finally, Mike Sabock, the special teams coach at Northern Illinois University, writes about developing the special teams unit. A lot of effort goes into creating a successful special teams unit, and Coach Sabock covers the topic from every angle, from personnel selection to practice time, organization, and coaching responsibilities. He includes coaching points, game preparation, and a grading system.

These successful coaches have contributed their expertise to this section on tactics. The information they provide will give you insight into how they approach these phases of the kicking game, insight you will find very helpful in developing your own special teams units.

CHAPTER 1

© Eric Evans

PUNTS

ROBIN ROSS
University of Oregon

The punting team is the most important team in football. Punting is the most-used special teams play, and punt execution determines field position for the defense and offense. The average net punt in college football is 35 yards—no offensive play can consistently average anything close to that many yards. The punting unit can turn a game around. A saying we use with all our special teams is "field position + momentum = points." This formula holds true in all football contests.

In this chapter, we will cover all aspects of punting the football—protection, coverage, red-zone punts, coming-out punts, and running fakes to make the opposing defense cover receivers and to account for base-run and option responsibilities.

Punting can be an effective weapon, but it can also be devastating if it is not properly executed. A blocked punt can turn field position around or lead to points; in 90 percent of games in which a punt is blocked, the team that is blocked loses the game. A good punt return can be just as devastating and lead to points for your opponent. It is impossible to place too much importance on punt execution.

When evaluating the punting team, the most important statistic is net punt. This is the distance from your line of scrimmage to the point at which the opponent takes possession of the football. The distance the ball goes does not dictate field position; rather, hang time is the key to increased net punting distance. The longer the ball is in the air, the farther the coverage players have to go to get to the punt returner. Your punter must understand the importance of hang time and not measure his success according to gross punting yards.

The punter needs a complete understanding of the team's punting philosophy every time he goes on the field. It is critical to have a coach assigned to the punter to emphasize the punter's role. Make sure the punter understands how important his contribution is to the success of the team. Often punters who do not play an offensive or defensive position don't feel they are a part of the team and don't fully appreciate their contribution. An easy way to remedy this is to have the head coach be the punters position coach. The head coach always sets the priorities for the team. When the head coach takes an active part in the punting team, the entire team will understand the importance of this special team.

Punting Personnel

Selecting the right players is the key to any successful team, and the punting team is no exception. When selecting your punting team, keep in mind the statistics mentioned earlier: Punts consistently net about 35 yards, and a team that has a punt blocked is likely to lose the game.

Special teams always start with the specialists. The snapper and punter are the foundation on which you build your punting team. Next in importance is the personal protector. He is the player who quarterbacks the punting team. He must be able to handle any situation that might occur.

All players selected for the punting team must have a strong sense of responsibility. We need players we can count on to do their job. We need players who are intelligent, who know what to do and how to do it.

The punter must be a perfectionist. His athletic ability will determine whether or not you can run fakes and how well he handles a bad snap. If his throwing is poor, he must practice throwing every day, even during the off-season, until he becomes a functional passer. He must have a strong leg and be able to get good hang time and distance.

The snapper must also be a perfectionist. Look for a player with a tight end, defensive end, linebacker, or fullback body type; a player of this size will take up space on the line. The player must be able to snap the ball 15 yards in less than 0.8 seconds plus step back and block a gap. The next section covers the snapper in more detail.

The personal protector must be able to identify the fronts he will face and call the right protection. He must be good at making decisions and conscientious enough to study the opponent. Look for a player with a fullback, tight end, middle linebacker, or strong safety body type. This player must be physically able to block two rushers if necessary, but he also must be mentally prepared to take ownership of the punting team and assume a leadership role.

Gunners must be able to release from the line of scrimmage to be the primary tacklers. Defensive backs, wide receivers, and running backs usually have the skills and speed necessary in these positions.

Guards must have the size to protect and not be overpowered or pulled. They are the closest players to the center gap and must help the center with his spacing. Look for players with tight end, defensive end, linebacker, or fullback body types. Guards must be able to cover and tackle.

Tackles must have the size to protect and the agility to release, cover, and keep leverage on the returner. Look for players with tight end, linebacker, strong safety, or fullback body types. Tackles must be able to tackle and cover.

Wings must be athletic enough to force a wide rusher around the punter and strong enough to stop the power rush and contain the returner. A strong safety, quick linebacker, big wide receiver, or fullback would be a good choice, but he must have the speed to keep the returner from getting around a corner near the sideline.

Punting Unit Tips and Reminders

1. Be ready. Watch for the punt alert on the third down. Get set quickly.

2. Personal protector: Count heads to make sure only 11 players are on the field. Set up 5 yards from the line of scrimmage except when the ball is inside the 5-yard line. Never set up deeper than 2 yards in the end zone.

3. Execute good splits and stances. Gunners: Make sure you are on the line. Key the ball and be careful not to jump early.

4. Guards, tackles, and gunners: Helmets must break the plane of the center's belt line.

5. Gunners: Come inside the numbers and then split out.

6. Wings: Contain except on a switch with a tackle.

7. Do not follow a teammate downfield.

8. Keep the ball inside and in front (shoulder force).

9. Respect the returner's opportunity for a fair catch. Be in position to recover in case the returner drops the ball. Even if the returner bobbles the ball, do not make contact with him if he has called for a fair catch. Do not go after the ball until it touches the ground.

10. Be ready to down the ball inside the 10-yard line.

11. When downing a punt, do not allow any part of the ball to come in contact with the goal line or break the plane of the goal line.

12. Anyone on the punting team can catch and down the punt provided that no one from the receiving team is in the vicinity trying to catch the ball.

13. Be aware of the clock. Always know the direction of the wind. At the end of the first or third quarter, be prepared to use the clock to take advantage of kicking with the wind.

14. Center and personal protector: Know when the clock is inside two minutes and let the time run down before the snap. If the punt hits the ground, let it roll and then cover it.

Punt Snaps

There is no fundamental distinction between punt snaps and PAT snaps. Only the target is different. The long snapper needs to focus and snap to the target.

To warm up, the long snapper should run through these drills:

- Complete overhead throws with another player, first from 5 yards away, then from 10 yards away.
- Complete overhead throws while kneeling. In these first two drills, emphasize quick arm extension and cocking of the wrists. The snapper should turn the palms out, letting the ball come off the first two fingers as they point toward the target. Extension of the arm must power the ball, not the wrists. If the ball doesn't spiral, it is probably because the long snapper is using the wrist too much in the throwing motion. Finally, have a specific target.
- Squat in snapping position. Be sure the feet are even, the ball is placed correctly in the middle, and the wrists are cocked. The snapper goes through the snapping motion without releasing the ball. All power must come from the snapper's body—he must generate all action by pushing off the toes. The knees should be bent as much as possible. The snapper must drive both forearms through his thighs.

There are several techniques essential to a good snap. The long snapper must learn these essentials and practice them often. First, he visualizes proper body position when addressing the ball. The feet should be parallel and at a comfortable width. They should also be even; use yard lines or hash marks as a guide. His weight is on the balls of the feet and the heels are slightly elevated. Knees are bent and the back is straight, preferably parallel to the ground. The ball is far enough in front of the snapper that he has to extend his arms to reach it, but he should still be able to maintain a squatting position with his back straight. The ball should be extended in front of the snapper's nose (or in front of the off-hand eye). The snapper puts his off hand on a seam perpendicular to the ground. Wrists are cocked at or near 90 degrees. The throwing hand is flexed under the ball. The off hand is hyperextended on top of the ball. The first or second finger of the off hand is on the perpendicular seam.

Second, the snapper focuses on the target. He visualizes the perfect snap to a specific spot on the punter (usually the kicking hip, belt buckle, or hands) or the holder (usually the hands or inside shoulder).

Third, the snapper lets his body do the snapping. The hands only direct the ball to the target; the snapper generates movement by pushing off the toes. He tries to keep his back straight as his feet glide over the turf by maintaining some bend in the knees. He drives both forearms through his thighs. Both palms are turned out, and the ball comes off the first fingers of both hands. The first fingers should be on the same level and at the same depth, pointing directly at the target as the ball comes off the hands.

Fourth, the snapper works to get depth on the snap. He shuffles to the right or left as called by the personal protector. He blocks the defender in his area, trying to stay as square as possible, and then he releases and goes into coverage.

Having flat feet, hopping, or beginning a snap with the arms instead of the feet result in short snaps. Falling forward or completely straightening the legs result in a high snap because the snapper's rear end shoots up. A wobbly snap usually is the result of the snapper using the wrist to throw the ball instead of driving the forearms through the legs. Uneven (nonparallel) feet when addressing the ball or at the end of the snap, uneven fingers at the release, or improper ball placement when addressing the ball can cause a one-handed snap. Curve balls usually occur when the seams of the ball are not perpendicular to the ground or when the snapper addresses the ball off center and consciously or subconsciously compensates as he snaps.

Punting Goals and Procedures

The punting team averages more plays per game than any other special team, so consistent punt execution is crucial. Through repetition, effort, and desire, the punting game can become a successful part of the overall game plan.

Our philosophy is to kick the ball as quickly as possible, provide solid protection, and cover quickly. We must never allow any protection breakdowns, which could give the receiving team the opportunity to block the punt. We must never allow any long returns.

Protecting the punter is the first priority, followed by covering the punt. Expect an all-out rush every time so you are not surprised when it happens. Discipline and concentration are the keys to accomplishing this goal.

Finally, success requires a high degree of communication, coordination, and skill. The players on this team are chosen for their athletic skills and their ability to concentrate and perform under pressure.

At Oregon we establish goals and procedures for the punting team. Here are our punting team goals:

- No blocked punts.
- No punts returned for touchdowns.
- Net punting average of 38 yards.
- Average punt return of 4 yards or less.
- Average hang time of 4.5 seconds or more.
- Average punt of 42 yards or more.
- Turnover created.

On all third downs, except when we are in field goal range, we make the call on the sideline: Punt team be ready. We attempt to move the ball to midfield. The punting team huddles at the sideline near the 50-yard line. The coach and players make sure all 11 players are accounted for. The personal protector calls out the type of coverage and repeats it, such as "Base coverage, base coverage," followed by "Punt on center's snap, ready, break." A designated player passes on the calls to players on the punting team who were on the field for third down. Players clap their hands and yell "Break." When the ball is in the red zone, the personal protector tells the huddle, "Red-zone punt." When the personal protector breaks the huddle, both gunners turn to the punter, make eye contact, and say "Red zone."

On fourth down, the punting team hustles to the field. They go directly to the line of scrimmage and get in formation as quickly as possible (figure 1.1). The personal protector counts to make sure all 11 players are on the field.

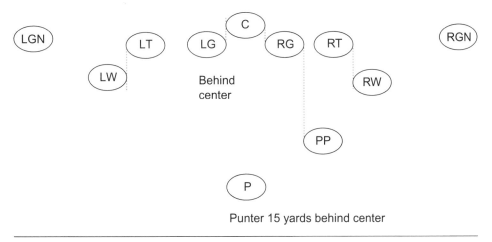

Figure 1.1 Punting formation and alignment.

The punter lines up 15 yards behind the center. The guard's inside toe is 6 inches outside and behind the center's heel. The tackle's inside toe is parallel with the guard's. The width between the tackle and the guard is half an arm's length or about 18 inches. The wing's inside toe is directly behind the tackle's outside heel. He is generally about an arm's length back from the tackle's hip. The personal protector lines up 4 to 5 yards deep on the same side as the punter's kicking foot. The personal protector's inside leg is directly behind the guard's outside leg. If the ball is in the middle of the field, the gunners line up on the inside edge of the numbers (figure 1.2a). If the ball is on a hash mark, the gunner on the boundary side of the field lines up on the outside edge of the numbers

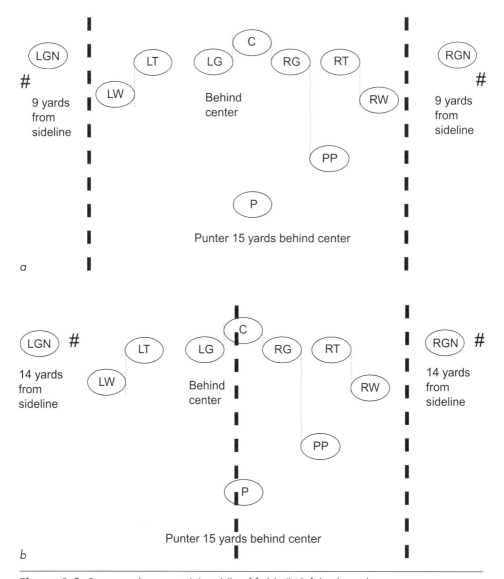

Figure 1.2 Gunners alignment: *(a)* middle of field; *(b)* left hash mark.

and the gunner on the wide side of the field lines up halfway between the numbers and the hash mark (figure 1.2b).

At the line of scrimmage, the personal protector makes a series of calls. He identifies the opponents, the number of potential rushers, and the type of punt rush alignment (balanced, overloaded, stacked, or safe). He tells the center which way to turn, right ("Ray") or left ("Lou"), and then says "Pause, set" to signal everyone to hold their position. For example, the personal protector might say, "Eight man, balanced, ray, pause, set."

When the center is ready, he snaps the ball. Often we have the personal protector hold the cadence and start with, for example, T minus 15 with the intent of snapping the ball at 5 seconds.

The timing of the punt play is important as well. When executing the snap-to-punt process, we adhere to these standards:

Snap (15 yards): 0.8 seconds

Punter's time: 1.3 seconds

Total time to kick: 2.1 seconds

If the sequence takes any longer than 2.1 seconds, we risk the possibility of a blocked punt or premature release by the coverage team.

Zone Protection

At the University of Oregon, we are a zone protection team. Splits and techniques are vital when a team uses this kind of protection. Players must keep their head up and focus on more than one man. They have to see the whole picture. Proper front recognition (who is in the box) allows the team to block any front.

In our zone protection scheme, we have designated lanes. Everyone has coverage responsibilities. Players must know and perfect the techniques required to properly execute their coverage.

Man protection depends on each player blocking a specific man. All techniques are the same as in zone protection, except at the collision point, the player releases his inside post hand and delivers a blow with both hands. In man protection, counting is from the outside in.

In contrast, the zone concept relies on three principles. First, each player protects the area from his inside leg to the inside leg of the next man to the outside. For instance, the area for a wing is from his inside leg to a spot 5 yards outside his alignment. Second, the concept of zone is to stay together, set together, and finish together, all at the same horizontal level (much like a picket fence). We use a vertical set and maintain a constant split relationship. Finally, zone protection uses techniques involving the hands. Players post with their inside hand and strike the widest threats in their zone with their outside hand.

The stack call is made between a guard and a tackle or between a tackle and a wing when one defender is on the line of scrimmage and another is high off the ball. Figure 1.3 shows a seven-man stack alignment to the right side.

The twist call (figure 1.4) is made between the tackle and the wing when two defenders align outside the tackle and on the line of scrimmage.

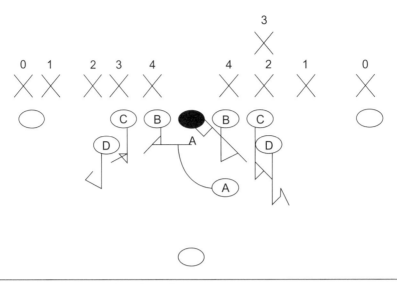

Figure 1.3 Seven-man stack to the right.

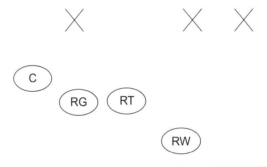

Figure 1.4 Twist call.

A creeper is any defender who starts his alignment over one of the gunners and then sneaks back inside toward the ball during the cadence. If there is only one creeper, the personal protector alerts the line to the creeper's presence. The players on the creeper's side will block out to the creeper. If there are creepers on both sides of the formation (figure 1.5), the personal protector will call "Check, Ray (or Lou), pause, then set." This call means everyone should hold on, start over, and recount from the outside in. The center always goes toward the Ray or Lou (right or left) call.

When the balance call is made, the center is responsible for any A-gap defender in the direction of the Ray or Lou call who loops across in front of the center. If the A-gap defender stays on the same A-gap side, the center stays with him. The personal protector is responsible for the A-gap defender (number 4 in figure 1.6) on the opposite side of the Ray

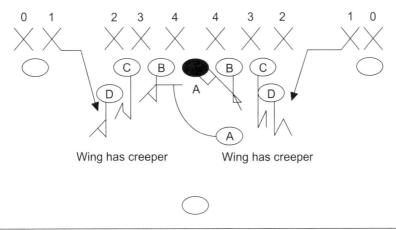

Figure 1.5 Six-man balanced Ray, double creeper.

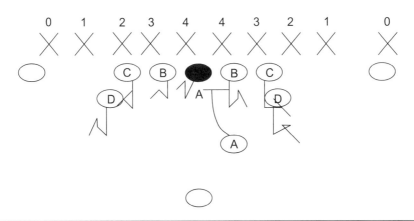

Figure 1.6 Eight-man balanced Lou.

or Lou call. Figure 1.6 shows a balanced eight-man alignment with a call to the left.

For the overload call, the personal protector must always turn the center toward the overloaded side. The center takes the A-gap toward the overloaded side (the Ray or Lou call tells him which side is overloaded) and does not follow any defenders who loop across in front of him. The personal protector is responsible for the looper because the personal protector is going to the A-gap in the opposite direction of the Ray or Lou call. If two players loop across in front of the center, the center takes the second looper and the personal protector takes the first. Figure 1.7 shows a seven-man overloaded alignment to the right side.

The personal protector makes the center stack call when a defender is head up, or shaded, over the center and another defender is aligned high, or off the ball, behind the man over the center. The personal protector should make the Ray or Lou call in the opposite direction of the man shading the center. If the man over the center is head-up, the personal protector turns the center in the direction of the punter's kicking leg with a Ray or Lou call. Figure 1.8 shows a center stack call to the left side against an eight-man alignment.

Against a seven-man front, someone will be free to serve as an extra protector. The personal protector should always turn the center toward the overloaded side. If the center has a man head-up in front of him, the personal protector makes the Ray or Lou call in the direction of the

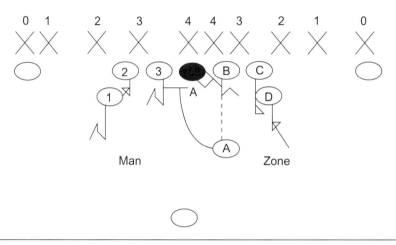

Figure 1.7　Seven-man overload Ray.

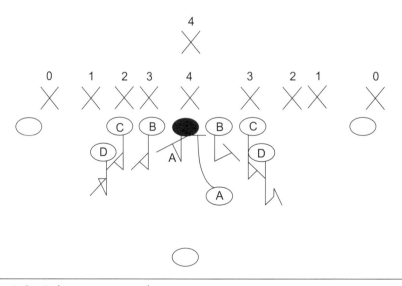

Figure 1.8　Eight-man center stack Lou.

punter's kicking leg and looks to protect the A-gap away from the call. Figure 1.9 shows a seven-man front with a call to the right.

Against a 9- or 10-man rush, the personal protector must recognize and point out the 9th or 10th rusher. The gunners and wings also will point out the 9th or 10th rusher. The punter is responsible for passing the ball to the uncovered receiver. During practice we work against a 10-man rush using the zone concept and get the ball off with the proper snap and zone principles.

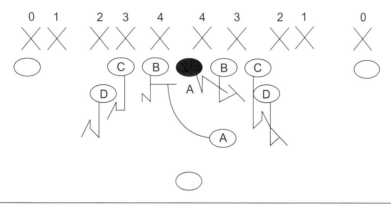

Figure 1.9 Seven-man Ray.

Punt Coverage Principles

In our zone coverage scheme, each player has specific coverage responsibilities. The basic rule is to never let the returner get to the player's outside shoulder. Players must keep the returner on their inside shoulder at all times (figure 1.10). Gunners take the fastest release possible, aiming for the returner's outside number. The personal protector gets his head up to the returner, reads the return, and goes to the ball. The center gets his head up on the returner. The guards get 5 yards outside the returner, the tackles get 10 yards outside the returner, and the wings get 15 yards outside the returner. The wings have containment responsibility. They scrape if the returner advances the ball in the opposite direction.

We teach our players several principles for covering punts. The first has already been mentioned: players must never let the returner get to their outside shoulder. They should keep the ball on the inside and tackle the ball with the inside shoulder.

We demand maximum effort from the punting team. Players must sprint 100 percent of the time. Anything less than 100 percent gives the return team the chance to beat us. Punt coverage is a total team effort. Only maximum effort by all 11 players is acceptable.

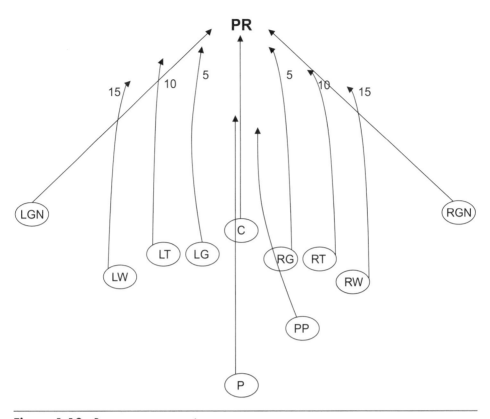

Figure 1.10 Return coverage assignments.

If a blocked punt does not cross the line of scrimmage, the ball is still in play. Either side may recover and advance the ball. If a blocked punt does pass the line of scrimmage, the kick is treated as any other punt. The return team can return the ball, so we must be prepared to tackle the returner. We must not touch a blocked punt that has crossed the original line of scrimmage unless we are downing a ball that has stopped rolling.

When releasing to cover a punt, players identify whether the opponent's return team is trying to rush the punt or hold us up. If they are attempting to hold us up, we use release techniques such as those used by the wide receivers and tight end or we use pass rush techniques such as swim, power underneath, slap hands off, or stick moves.

We instruct players to gather their feet at a point 10 yards from the returner. This means the player gets under control, lowers his hips, keeps his feet moving, gets in hitting position, stays square, and comes to balance.

Players are taught to never follow their own color (teammates). If a player finds himself directly behind a teammate, he must move 5 yards to the outside or inside. This results in the proper field distribution. Initially the coverage fans out to cover the field. Once the ball is caught, however, everyone converges on the returner. We always try to intimidate the opponent's returner with gang tackling and fierce hitting, and we always try to create a fumble.

Players must give the returner a chance to catch the ball. If the returner signals for a fair catch, players get in front of the returner with their palms up so they can scoop up a bobbled or fumbled punt.

Punts not fielded by the opponent's returner must be circled when rolling in our favor. When the ball stops rolling, a player picks up the ball and hands it to an official. When the ball is rolling in the opponent's favor, a player downs it and gives it to an official. If the ball is rolling into the end zone, a player jumps, dives for the ball, bats it away, or does whatever is necessary to keep the ball from entering the end zone. A punt downed inside the 5-yard line is a tremendous momentum boost and could help us win the game.

Punts in Special Circumstances

Although all punts are important, punts in the red zone and backed-up punts are special challenges for the punting team. How well we execute these special punts helps determine our overall success in the game.

For the red-zone punt (figure 1.11), the center (snapper) covers straight to the ball. When the returner signals fair catch, the center breaks down 3 yards from the returner. The personal protector also releases straight to the ball and breaks down 3 yards from the returner. The guards have the same coverage responsibilities as usual. They also break down 3 yards from the returner. On a fair catch, however, they must be alert to recovering a fumble or muff.

The tackles and wings have the same coverage responsibilities as usual. They, too, need to be alert to a possible fumble on an attempted fair catch. If necessary, they need to prevent the ball from going into the end zone. The gunner to the side of the punt goes behind the returner, looks for the ball, and protects the goal line. The gunner away from the side of the punt defines the punt and goes to either the returner or the goal line, depending on the flight of the ball. In the red zone, we may catch the ball if the returner does not attempt a catch. We must down the ball on the field of play, preferably within the 10-yard line.

Teams use a backed-up punt (figure 1.12) when ball placement doesn't allow the punter the full 15 yards to kick the ball. The punter aligns his heels 1 foot from the end line and must not step back. The personal protector aligns his heels 5 yards from the tip of the ball and must not step

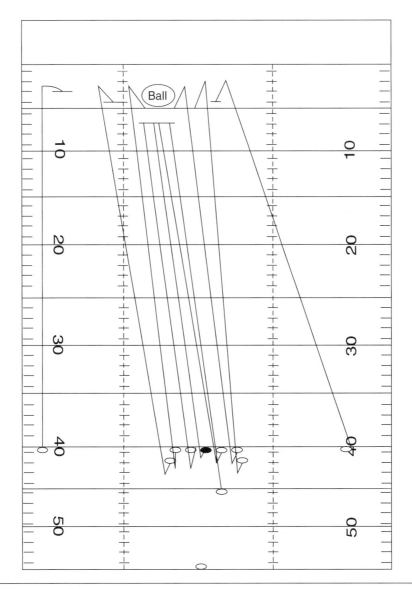

Figure 1.11 Red-zone punt.

back. He must also remind the punter to watch the end line. The rest of the punting team assume their normal splits (splits can be adjusted according to game plan) and alignments, getting maximum depth off the ball. Players take only one step on a rail with the outside foot and strike through the outside gap. They must not leave until they hear the thump of the ball; then they sprint into their coverage. The ball is punted from 7 yards deep rather than 9 or 10 yards deep. The protection cup must be solid inside. The tackles and wings must have less depth to compensate for the angle of the outside rushers.

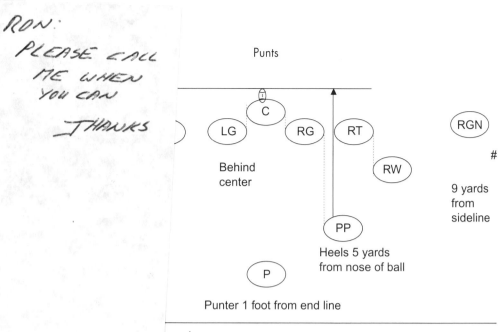

RON:
PLEASE CALL
ME WHEN
YOU CAN

THANKS

Punts

C

LG   RG   RT   RGN

#

Behind center

RW

9 yards from sideline

PP

Heels 5 yards from nose of ball

P

Punter 1 foot from end line

punt.

Practice and Drills

Efficiency is the most important thing to keep in mind when organizing practice. Special teams require a tremendous amount of organization because they use players and coaches from both sides of the ball. Written practice plans can help organize punt practice and help the coaches who are working with the punting team. The team should practice punts every day for a minimum of 10 minutes, resulting in 40 minutes of punt practice per week. You may need to adjust your schedule slightly from week to week, but a set routine usually works best for players and coaches. Players practice better when they know what to expect, and drills become more efficient because it takes less time to set them up. Another great time to work on punt coverage or red-zone punts is during conditioning. This can be a reward for players on the punting team and can emphasize a particular aspect of the punting game.

Punting team meetings also can be beneficial. This time is valuable because it allows you to improve the quality of your practice time on the field. A 10-minute review of the last game at the following practice and a 15-minute meeting again a couple of days later can set the tone for practice as well as become a great teaching tool. Again the key is efficiency. Position coaches understand the importance of the punting team but often feel this time could be better spent on offense or defense. If you are efficient and organized both in meetings and on the field, you will ensure that all coaches are involved and time is used effectively.

The breakdown of each coach's responsibilities is vital. To maximize time on the field and coaching techniques, each coach should be responsible for no more than three positions. This allows each coach to be more productive. Coaching special teams should be approached in a similar manner to coaching offense or defense. Coaches not working with the punting team can help run the practice squad, giving players the best picture of what they will see in a game. Here is how we break down each coach's responsibility:

Head coach: Punter

Offensive line coach: Snapper

Special teams coordinator: Personal protector

Wide receivers or defensive backs coach: Gunners

Wide receivers or defensive backs coach: Gunners practice squad

Inside linebackers coach: Right guard, tackle, and wing

Running backs coach: Right guard, tackle, and wing practice squad

Outside linebackers coach: Left guard, tackle, and wing

Defensive assistant: Left guard, tackle, and wing practice squad

This format allows the assistant offensive line coach to work with the offensive line and the defensive line coach to work with the defensive line. It also gives the quarterbacks coach time to work with players not involved with the punting team. This schedule keeps the entire team involved in special teams practice, either with the punting team, the offense, or the defense, or by serving the punting team through the practice squads.

The weekly practice schedule covers all situations that may occur during a punt:

Monday: Review game tape

Tuesday: 10-minute practice (5 minutes half-line work with coaches on the week's blocks; gunner work on release techniques against holdups; 5 minutes team work versus all blocks, punt, and cover, which is taped for Wednesday's meeting)

Wednesday: 15-minute meeting to show blocks and returns, viewing practice tape from Tuesday; 10-minute practice (5 minutes team versus blocks when the ball is on the 2-yard line coming out, 5 minutes team red-zone punt from hash marks)

Thursday: 10-minute practice (work with core players on snaps, fakes, special plays)

Friday: 10-minute video review of blocks and returns used by the upcoming opponent; 10-minute walk-through of all possible game situations

Although not all of these situations arise in every game, preparing players for any situation helps you win games. In a game I coached about 10 years ago, a simple thing such as going over the rules of a blocked punt the night before the game led to a win. The opposing team partially blocked our punt and the ball crossed the line of scrimmage. The opposing team touched the ball. In unison our punting team went to recover the ball and hand it to the official, calling our ball. The opposing team was in shock. We took advantage of the field position and momentum. The team turned this one play into points to win the game.

Protection drills begin with players on field lines in the proper stance with hands on knees. The drills work on kick slides on the movement of the ball. Players post punch with their inside hand, thumb up. They push off their inside foot and reach back with their outside foot. Their eyes focus on the outside area of protection. Drills must be done on a line for reference to straight-back vertical set and constant split relationship.

The next progression of the kick slide drill is to put two defenders opposite each man and have them rush straight ahead. Each protector gets a post punch on the inside man and uses both hands to strike through the outside man with the hands in position on the numbers. They make contact with the outside rusher on the line.

For the gunners drill, the gunners begin in a two-point stance with the inside foot up. Each gunner has a holdup man in front of him. The gunner works to release against the holdup man. Releases are the same as the wide receiver's release. Gunners always work to half of the holdup man, using an arm-under or arm-over move to get around the man. Set up cones 10 yards downfield to get the gunner back in his lane after his release, recapturing the ground he lost on his move around the holdup man.

The leverage tackle drill focuses the two gunners on keeping proper leverage on the returner. The gunners are the primary coverage players and have no protection responsibilities; they must always maintain leverage outside the returner. The gunners align 2 yards outside the hash marks. A coach and a returner line up 20 yards away in the middle of the field. On the coach's command, the gunners move to the returner. When the gunners are 10 yards from the returner, the coach gives the ball to the returner. The returner tries to avoid the gunners by moving up the field or around the outside.

A team coverage drill (figure 1.13) can be used as a half-line drill to start and put together a full team. This drill is useful for teaching coverage responsibilities and lane relationships when covering punts in different areas of the field.

The coach and returner stand 40 yards away from the line of scrimmage. The punting team assumes their alignment at the line. The ball is snapped and punted against air. (The punt is not fielded.) The gunners release when the ball is snapped. The front line takes two kick slides into their setups and release to the returner. The gunners and personal protector sprint to

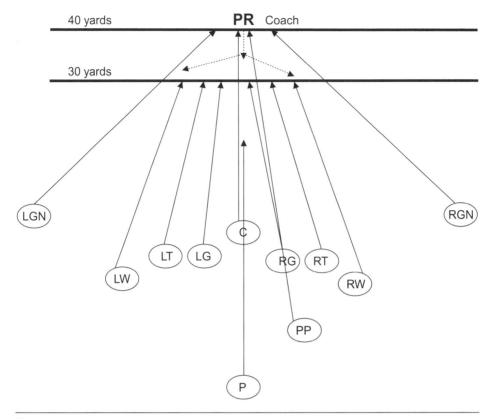

Figure 1.13 Team coverage.

the returner and break down around him. The center, guards, tackles, and wings break down 10 yards from the returner with 4-yard spacing. The coach hands the ball to the returner. When the first wave of coverage has broken down around the returner, they let the returner run to the second wave 10 yards away and try to leverage the second wave. All players in the second wave should keep proper leverage on the returner and their outside foot back and their shoulders square. When the ball moves away, they should fold to pick up pursuit angles on the ball.

CHAPTER 2

© Human Kinetics

KICKOFFS

GREG MCMAHON
University of Illinois

Kickoff coverage is a vital part of a team's quest to control field position. When you pin an opponent deep in his own territory, you dictate his offensive options. If your opponent is forced to start the possession inside his own 20-yard line, his chances of scoring greatly diminish.

For the coverage team to be successful, each man must carry out his assignment. Successful kickoff coverage is a team effort. Intense effort and desire are also part of a successful kickoff team. In addition to effort and desire, players in this unit all have speed, toughness, agility, and football sense.

Each player must stay in his assigned lane as he locates the ball. They can adjust lanes relative to the ball. Players must not cross the ball. A player who starts right of the ball needs to stay right of the ball, keeping the ball on the proper shoulder. Also, players look to make the big play. A player who finds an opening closes it, squeezing to the ball relative to the player to his inside. Players always tackle the ball carrier's outside leg.

When approaching a blocker, the player gets by him as quickly as possible. He can shoulder rip by the blocker, swim over him, put a move on him, or use a two-hand shiver. He must set up the blocker and run at the blocker to get him to set his feet. The player uses a two-hand punch and gets back into his lane. Each player needs to exercise common sense.

When taking on a blocker 10 yards or closer to the ball, the player fronts him and squeezes him to the football. He executes the butt and press. A player must not break down unless he is within 10 yards of the ball.

A player facing a wedge must never trade one for one. He needs to take at least two with him. He fills in the proper gap when taking on the wedge and stays high—this is a rule. A player facing a double team holds his lane responsibility. If he gets knocked down, he comes up running.

The Getoff

Hitting the 35-yard line at a full sprint is the key to our coverage. We want our coverage team to have a reputation for team tackling. When they hold the runner up, they try to strip the ball loose. Our goal is to hold the opponent's return average under 18 yards, tackling the ball carrier inside the 20-yard line. If the kick has a hang time of 4.0 seconds and is caught at the goal line, the coverage unit should be at the 30-yard line when the ball is caught.

When covering kicks, remember that collisions are good when your players are the ones creating them. Teach players to attack potential blockers; they must not wait for blockers to set their feet.

When we use a holder, we kick from the middle to away from the holder's side because it can be difficult for the holder to fill back in his lane.

To evaluate coverage, we stand at the line of scrimmage when the ball is kicked. At 20 yards we want to see a straight wall of defenders covering at full speed. When the ball is caught, the coverage team should be less than 30 yards from the returner.

Players must always anticipate that the returner will bring the ball out of the end zone. If the returner instead kneels in the end zone for a touchback, we want our coverage team to meet him there. All 11 players must sprint to the end zone.

Personnel Decisions

When choosing players for the kickoff coverage team, we look for specific body types.

The #1 position player must be able to run. He will be an aggressive safety. A defensive back or wide receiver is best suited to this position. He doesn't have to be huge, but he must be a sound tackler.

The #2 position player must be able to run well enough to squeeze blocks and be aggressive enough to take on kick-out blocks. A strong safety or big, physical wide receiver is ideal for this position.

The #3 position player must be big enough to take on double teams and wedge blocks. Speed is a factor if the return is away. A defensive back, fast linebacker, or fullback is best suited to this position.

The #4 and #5 position players must have good bulk and strength. They are closest to the kicker and the point of attack, so they must be stout enough to take on blocks and not get knocked out of their lanes. They see a lot of wedge blocking schemes. Linebackers and tight ends are best at the #4 and #5 positions.

The kicker needs to approach the ball consistently so that the coverage team can time their approach for the getoff. We like for the kicker to be within 9 yards of the ball, but that can be adjusted. If the kick is not a touchback, we have a goal of a 4.0 hang time to the goal line. The shorter the kick, the more hang time the ball must have.

Phases of Kickoff Coverage

Proper kickoff coverage begins with the getoff and ends with preventing a long return.

For the getoff, each player must key into the kicker's approach and match his approach to the kicker's tempo. By the time he hits the line of scrimmage, he should be at a full sprint. This is called the all-out zone. Remind players not to be offside. If the men can coordinate their getoff, they will avoid vertical gaps in the coverage.

Lane distribution is the next part of kickoff coverage. The horizontal gaps between players must be 5 to 6 yards wide. These gaps must remain constant. Players that are too far apart or too close together create seams that are too big to be filled. If a player gets knocked out of his lane while avoiding a block, he must work hard to get back into his lane. Remind players to never follow a teammate down the field. The man in the trail position must adjust to fill in the void. Any player who gets knocked down must get up and fill in the void. Players must never stay on the ground.

Each player needs to be aware of the return scheme. Each position is assigned an awareness key before the snap. The drops of the front blockers will tell a lot about the return scheme. Players must not allow the front blockers to force them to break down too soon. If the blockers on the kicking team attempt to block early, players must avoid the block and get back into their lanes. This is called the avoid zone.

A player within 10 to 15 yards of the returner begins to break down. He attacks the block, being careful not to pick an edge. He stays square and reestablishes the line of scrimmage. This is called the attack zone.

If the front blockers on the kicking team do not attempt to block, the player swivels his head to watch out for kick-out or kick-in blocks. He also needs to look for a deep wedge.

Remind players to never give up one for one—always force double teams. A double team will free up another coverage man.

Players should squeeze all returns. As blockers go away, players begin to restrict their lanes. They must not restrict too early or they will lose the proper spacing with the other coverage men. Reduce the field for the return as much as possible, but never give up lane integrity to do so.

Remind players to always keep the ball inside. They need to keep proper leverage on the ball at all times. This means keeping the ball inside and in front. Players should always take on blocks with the inside arm and keep the outside arm free.

Huddle and Alignments

The kicker positions the ball at the 35-yard line in the middle of the field. (In high school and youth leagues, the ball is placed at the 40-yard line.) For a safety kick, he puts the ball on the 20-yard line. The left side of the kickoff team is the front wall. They align at the 25-yard line. The right side aligns behind the left side at the 24-yard line (see figure 2.1).

The kicker counts to 11. He addresses the team and calls the kick, such as "Deep middle, deep middle, ready, break." Players break the huddle sharply and hustle to their assigned position. After the referee blows the whistle to begin play, the kicker simultaneously shouts "Ready!" and raises his arm. This sets the team and puts the game in the kicker's control.

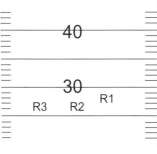

The Official 365 Sports Facts-A-Year Calendar

n, starting at the 25-yard
foot on the 25-yard line.
ward the ball with their
nan they are facing. Each
inside. R1 and L1 split 4

mes use kickoff coverage
ne and the ball is kicked

Zones

The three zones of kickoff coverage are the all-out zone, the avoid zone, and the attack zone (figure 2.2). In the all-out zone, players get off at the line of scrimmage at 20 yards. They must not allow vertical or horizontal seams.

L1: 5 yards from sideline

L2: On numbers

L3: Split numbers and hash mark

L4: Hash mark

L5: 5 yards from hash mark

On the right side, splits mirror the left side.

In the attack zone, players use the butt and press. They should never get on the edge of blocks; instead they fit in the wedge and reestablish the line of scrimmage.

In the avoid zone, players cross the face of their assigned blockers, avoiding them with a hard turn. They quickly get back in their lanes.

There are three ways to defeat a blocker: cross his face (avoid zone; figure 2.3a); avoid him and make a hard turn (avoid zone; figure 2.3b); and

3 Areas of Kickoff Coverage

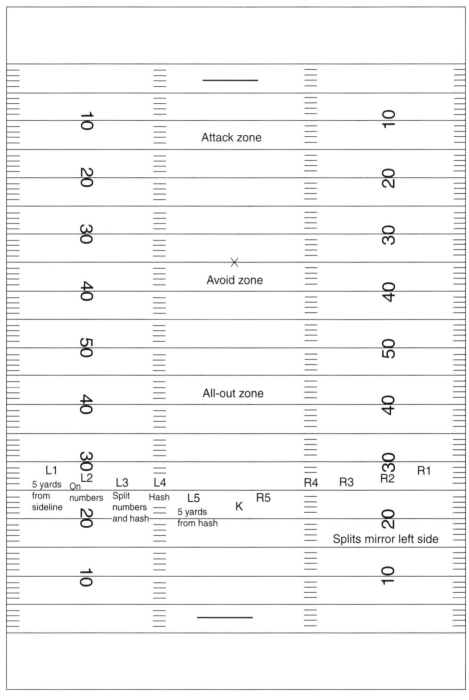

Figure 2.2 Three zones of kickoff coverage.

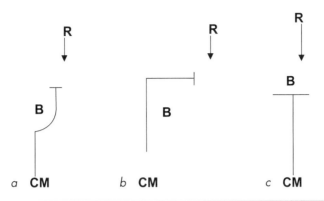

Figure 2.3 Three ways to defeat a blocker: *(a)* cross the face; *(b)* avoid and hard turn; *(c)* butt and press. CM = coverage man; B = blocker; R = returner.

use the butt and press (attack zone when the blocker cannot be avoided; figure 2.3c).

Awareness keys help players understand the opponent's blocking schemes. Each player must fully understand his keys. Here are the awareness keys for kickoff coverage for each position:

5: C–G

4: G–C

3: G–T

2: T–E

We emphasize several coaching points. If a player clears the front line unblocked, he should get his head on a swivel and look for kick-out or kick-in blocks. All players must keep the ball on their inside shoulder. When the blocker sets his feet, the players should attack him at full speed and punch. Everyone should get to the 30-yard line before adjusting lanes unless they are engaged in a block. Everyone should find the direction of the ball.

We also instruct players on where they fit in a middle wedge (figure 2.4). Players 5 and 4 (R and L) attack through the gaps using their outside shoulder. They should force the ball carrier to spill, and they must not

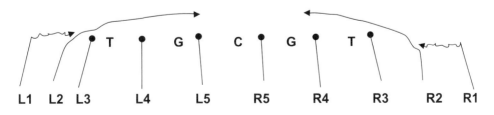

Figure 2.4 Middle wedge alignment.

let the ball go down the pipe. Players 5 and 4 must not get single blocked. Player 3 (R and L) penetrates through the outside shoulder of the blocker. He uses the inside shoulder pad to pin the ball carrier, preventing him from getting outside. He scrapes over the top if the ball is going away from them. Player 2 (R and L) must remember that his role is to contain. He always takes on blocks with his inside shoulder. If player 2 can beat the wedge outside to get the ball carrier, he takes it. He must squeeze all returns. Player 1 (R and L) acts as an aggressive safety. He keeps all blocks to the inside. He is a contain player when the ball is coming to him and a fold player when the ball is going away.

Types of Kicks

The type of kick used depends on the game situation, our personnel, our general philosophy for the kicking game, weather conditions, the opponent, and a variety of other factors. Middle kicks, directional kicks, mortar kicks, squib kicks, kicks after a safety, and onside kicks all have a part in the game. The kicking unit must be prepared for each of these calls.

The middle kick is our base scheme; barring bad weather or a great returner, we use this kick. We often use the directional kick to kick away from a great returner. When kicking into a strong wind, when kicking during bad weather, or when avoiding the main returner, we use the mortar kick to the right. We might also use this kick at the end of the first half or the game. We use the squib kick when weather conditions, such as strong wind, rain, or snow, prevent us from using a normal deep kick.

Middle Kick

For a kick down the middle of the field (figure 2.5), player 1 works in conjunction with player 2. Player 1 contains to the outside of 2 if the ball spills outside. If the ball comes inside, 2 and then 1 fill where needed. If the ball goes away, 1 plays cutback safety. Player 1 sprints to the 30-yard line 5 yards to the inside, keeping the ball inside and in front. Player 1 does his work between the 30- and 25-yard lines. He stacks and stays, never crossing the ball. Players 1 and 2 stay outside the blocks. They are responsible for reverses and throw-backs.

Player 2 is responsible for containment. He must be aggressive and squeeze down the formation, staying outside blocks. He must never cross the ball. On a play away, he folds.

Players 3, 4, and 5 sprint straight down the field. They get to the 30-yard line before adjusting lanes unless they are already engaged in a block. They fight double teams on their landmark.

All players attack blockers using a two-hand punch in order to get blockers to set their feet. Everyone needs to read their awareness keys

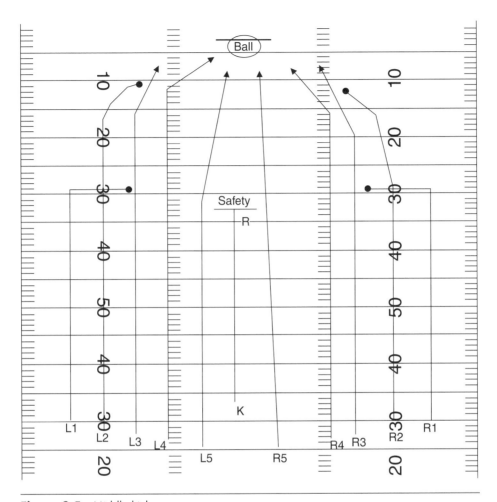

Figure 2.5 Middle kick.

and be aware of the return scheme. If the key goes away, the player scans the area for kick-out and kick-in blocks. All players must keep the ball on the inside shoulder and in front.

The kicker sprints down the field and fills inside the 30-yard line. We want the kicker to be aggressive and show color to the returner, providing one more defender for the returner to confront. The kicker must be part of the coverage unit.

Directional Kick

For a directional kick to the left of the field (figure 2.6), L1 is 5 yards from the sideline. He contains if the flow comes toward him and folds if the flow moves away from him. L2 covers down the numbers to his side. L3 goes directly to the ball. He is a ball hawk. L4's coverage lane is halfway

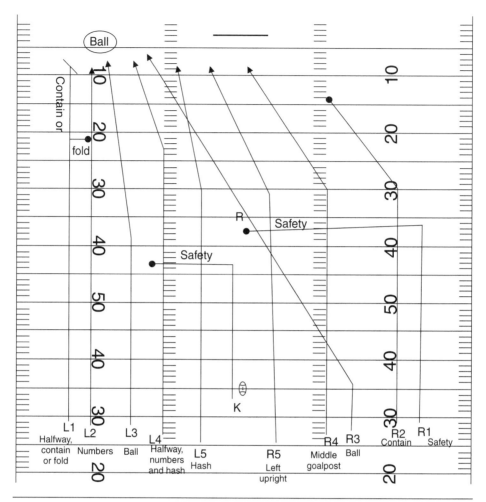

Figure 2.6 Directional kick to the left.

between the numbers and the hash mark. L5's coverage lane is down the left hash mark. R5's coverage lane is the left upright. He contains any returns to his side.

On the right side of the field, R4's coverage lane is the middle of the goalposts. He contains any returns to his side. R3 covers directly to the ball. He is a ball hawk. R2 executes a squeeze on the return. He must not cross the right hash mark. He contains any returns to his side. R1 is a safety. He covers to the 35-yard line and then settles down to contain from the outside in.

The kicker is a safety. He covers to the 40-yard line and settles down. He forces the ball back to the middle of the field.

A directional kick to the right mirrors a kick to the left.

Mortar Kick

For the mortar kick to the right (figure 2.7), R1 works 5 yards from the sideline. He contains if the flow comes toward him and folds if the flow moves away. R2 covers down the numbers to his side. R3 covers down his lane. The ball should be kicked directly in front of R3. R4 covers down his lane. The ball should be kicked slightly inside of R4. R5 covers down his lane. The ball is kicked to his outside. R5 must be prepared to squeeze the ball.

On the left side of the field, L5's coverage lane is the middle of the goalposts. He contains the ball to his inside. L4's coverage lane is the left upright. He contains the ball to his inside. L3 goes directly to the ball. He is a ball hawk. L2 squeezes the return. He must not cross the left hash

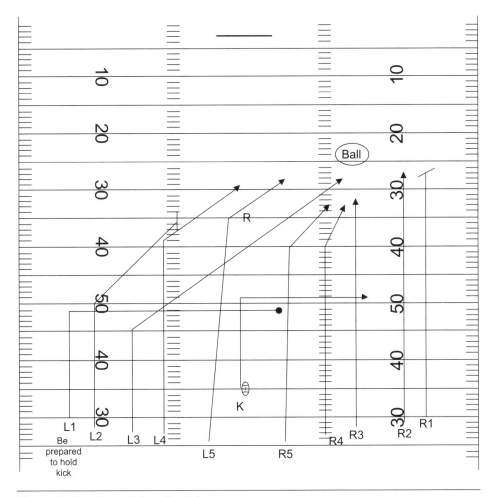

Figure 2.7 Mortar kick to the right.

mark. He contains any returns to his side. L1 is a safety. He covers to the 50-yard line and then contains from the outside in. L1 also needs to be prepared to hold for the kick if necessary.

The kicker kicks the ball between the 20- and 30-yard lines. The kick will have an abnormally high arc with an ideal hang time of more than 3.8 seconds. The kicker is a safety. He covers to the 50-yard line and settles. He forces the ball to the middle.

A mortar kick to the left mirrors a mortar kick to the right.

Squib Kick

The squib kick is the same as the middle kick with the exception of the kicker's responsibility. For a squib kick, the kicker executes a hard line-drive kick so that the ball bounces around the 30-yard line toward the end zone. Kickers should always be prepared for the squib kick call.

All principles of kickoff coverage apply to the squib kick. The coverage unit must be aware that blocks occur much more quickly with a squib kick. They will not be able to avoid blocks for as long and must get into the attack phase quickly. The second row handles the squib kick.

Depending on the situation, we may be willing to give up field position to disrupt the tempo of a return late in the first half of the game. We may also kick short or to the right or left to disrupt the return.

Kick After Safety

For a kickoff following a safety, the huddle sets on the 10-yard line. We use a straight-line formation. Lane responsibility, getoff, and coverage are the same as with a middle kick. The ball is kicked from the 20-yard line.

Either a punter or a kicker can kick off. A punter tends to have much better hang time than a kicker. However, depending on the weather and wind, a kicker may be the better choice. A punter's approach is different; he starts his approach on the 18-yard line. Work with the punter on timing.

The kick needs to have a 4.0 hang time or better. Coverage must be good enough to enable your team to regain field position. All kickoff rules and principles apply except you also have the option of punting the ball.

Onside Kick

For an onside kick to the left, players line up in the formation shown in figure 2.8. Players use a three-point stance. The three-point stance helps them reach full speed at the line of scrimmage and makes it easier to time the kick. The kicker lines up 2 to 3 yards from the football. Everyone else lines up on the 30-yard line.

When the kicker gives the "Ready" command and drops his hand to begin the kickoff, L1, L2, L3, L4, L5, and R5 begin their approach. R4, R3,

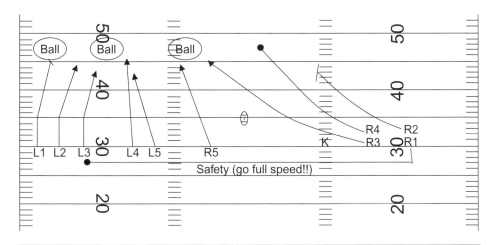

Figure 2.8   Onside kick to the left.

R2, and R1 take off as the kicker begins his approach. Everyone attempts to recover the ball. L1 must keep the ball in bounds. R2 does not cross the hash mark since he is the contain man. R1 must hustle to get into position as a safety. You can also use this kick to the right.

We use the surprise onside kick to the middle (figure 2.9) when we feel that a member of the front wall is vacating too quickly or uses abnormally wide splits. The kicker finds a bubble in the front row of the formation.

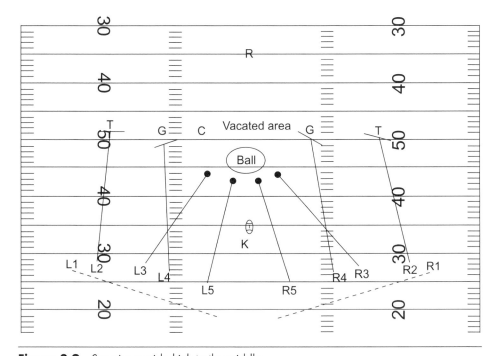

Figure 2.9   Surprise onside kick to the middle.

He short squibs the ball into the vacated area and recovers it himself. This takes great timing and precision. The tempo of the kicker's approach must remain the same as that of a normal kick in order to keep the element of surprise. To keep all players onside, you must work with them on the getoff. Slow down the approach. Players 2 and 4 block the most dangerous men after the ball goes 10 yards. Players 3 and 5 fold behind the ball. Player 1 becomes a safety.

Practicing Kickoff Coverage

Keep alignments and assignments simple. Most players have other offensive and defensive responsibilities to work on. Defeat your opponent with execution, not complicated schemes. Once you get out of fall camp, keep scheme changes to a minimum.

Players should work on the getoff in shorts and helmets. When working on the avoid and attack phases, players should wear helmets and shoulder pads. Players work at a thud tempo, where blocks are above the waist and the ball carrier is wrapped up but not brought to the ground. Collisions are live but not so hard they threaten anyone's safety.

We like to do all drill work in close quarters. There are no long running starts. Teach the players the techniques, but protect them from injury on the practice field.

Our game week begins on Sunday by passing out game grades and watching game tape. Then we take 5 minutes to work on getoffs at 20 yards, kickoffs after a safety (getoff), and onside kicks. On Tuesday, we hand out scouting reports for the upcoming game. We take 15 minutes to work on drills, getoffs, and basic schemes such as the middle kick and squib kick. On Thursday, we take 5 minutes to work on the onside kick and any special situations. On Friday, we hand out game-plan notes and take 10 minutes to work on the game script.

Here are a few of our kickoff coverage drills.

Getoff

The getoff drill (figure 2.10) simulates a gameday getoff. Players run through the all-out zone. The goal is to have all coverage men in a perfect line and even with the ball when it is kicked. The getoff drill is essential to learning proper timing.

Players on the coverage team, including the kicker, line up. You can do the getoff drill as either a full-team or half-line drill. No scouts are needed as this drill focuses only on the all-out zone.

Once the ball is teed up and all members of the coverage team are in their alignments, the kicker drops his hand or gives some other signal and approaches the ball. Each member of the coverage team is responsible

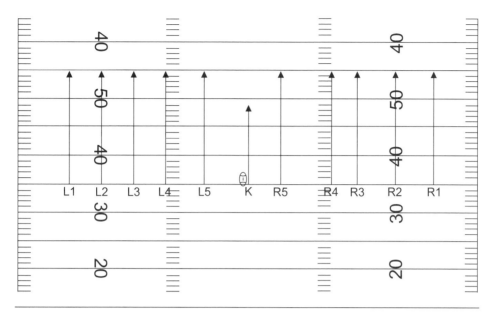

Figure 2.10 Getoff drill.

for timing his approach with the kicker; the kicker never has to adjust his speed. The coverage team hits the line at full speed as a unit just as the ball is kicked. From there, the drill is a 20-yard sprint with the goal of maintaining a straight line for all 20 yards. The getoff is measured at both the line of scrimmage and the opposite 45-yard line.

Avoid and Hard Turn

In the avoid and hard turn drill (figure 2.11) players practice what to do if a coverage man decides not to cross the face of a blocker in the avoid zone. The ability to make a hard turn toward the ball carrier is essential if a coverage man chooses to avoid a block rather than cross it.

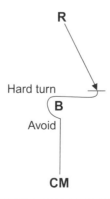

Figure 2.11 Avoid and hard turn drill. CM = coverage man; B = blocker; R = returner.

The drill is set up with one scout blocker holding a hand bag and one scout ball carrier positioned 10 yards directly behind him. The coverage man starts 5 yards from the scout blocker.

The coverage man runs at the blocker and uses a swim, rip, or other avoidance technique to defeat the blocker on a predetermined side. When the coverage man defeats the block, the ball carrier runs at a 45-degree angle to the other side. In order for the coverage man to get back to the ball, he must execute a hard turn. The coverage man works to get his head across when fitting up on the ball carrier.

Cross Face

The purpose of the cross face drill (figure 2.12) is to simulate the cross face technique, which is often used in the avoid phase in order to keep proper lane coverage. Crossing face is an alternative to the avoid and hard turn.

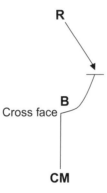

Figure 2.12 Cross face drill. CM = coverage man; B = blocker; R = returner.

One scout blocker holds a hand bag and one scout ball carrier positions himself 10 yards directly behind him. The coverage man starts 10 yards from the scout blocker.

The coverage man runs directly at the blocker. As the coverage man approaches, the ball carrier breaks one way or the other as predetermined by the coach. When the ball carrier breaks, the coverage man must read it and cross the blocker's face to get to the ball.

Butt and Press

The butt and press drill (figure 2.13) teaches players how to attack, control, and shed blockers in the attack zone.

With or without hand bags, scout blockers align 10 yards directly in front of the coverage men. A scout ball carrier sets up 20 yards behind the

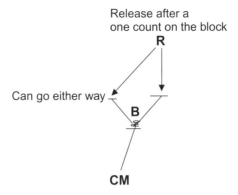

Figure 2.13 Butt and press drill. CM = coverage man; B = blocker; R = returner.

blockers. The ball carrier can be centered or to the left or right to simulate covering as a 1, 2, or 3 man or covering as a 4 or 5 man.

When the drill begins, the scout blockers take a 10-yard drop and set up to block. The coverage men run at and engage the scout blockers using a two-hand punch. The coverage men stay engaged momentarily while controlling the blocker. After a count of "One," the ball carrier is released and runs straight upfield. When the ball carrier breaks, the coverage men shed the scout blockers and work to fit up on the ball.

Weave

The weave drill (figure 2.14) accomplishes many things in a short amount of time. We use it to evaluate players as well as teach the basic fundamentals of avoiding and attacking blockers. It even includes breaking down and fitting up on a ball carrier. The weave drill incorporates techniques from all three zones of kickoff coverage (all-out, avoid, and attack).

In the weave drill players form lines on one sideline. Two scout players with hand bags set up on a given yard line. The first scout is aligned

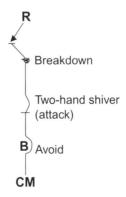

Figure 2.14 Weave drill. CM = coverage man; B = blocker; R = returner.

where the college numbers would be. The second scout is on the hash mark nearest the sideline where the drill begins. Scout ball carriers set up on the far college numbers to simulate fitting up on a returner.

A player runs full speed across the width of the field. The coverage man must avoid the first blocker using any of the avoidance techniques. He then uses a two-hand punch to shed the second scout blocker. After defeating the second block, the player must come to balance 10 yards in front of the scout ball carrier (use dots or cones for landmarks). Scout ball carriers run at a 45-degree angle in a predetermined direction once the coverage man has come completely to balance. The coverage man shuffles with the ball carrier and fits up on him, always putting his face mask on the outside of the ball carrier. The returner does not leave until the cover man has completely broken down.

Live Cover

The live cover drill simulates a gameday kickoff from start to finish. Thud tempo, in which everything but the tackle is live, helps prevent injuries.

The coverage team gets in their alignment and the ball is teed up. A full scout kickoff return team lines up, usually simulating an opponent's kickoff return formation.

The drill begins with a perfect getoff just as the ball is kicked. Then the coverage team goes through the all-out zone at full speed. When the coverage men enter the avoid zone, they must either cross the face of a scout blocker or avoid him and beat him with speed. After avoiding or crossing the face of a block, the coverage men execute their butt and press or fold techniques in the attack zone.

CHAPTER 3

© Human Kinetics

PUNT RETURNS

JOHN HARBAUGH
Philadelphia Eagles

As a football coach's son, I grew up believing that coaching and teaching are the greatest professions in the world. My dad coached high school and college ball for 43 years. He coached within some of the biggest rivalries, and as a head coach he won well over 100 games and a national championship. He played a positive role in the lives of countless young people, and many of those guys would say that he even saved them by giving them a chance to be better. But to me, the best thing he ever did was allow my brother and me to be a part of everything he did, whether we were kids running around next to practice or adults trying to help him build a better program. He gave me a chance to start out in coaching and continues to be a part of what I do every day.

It is with great pride that I offer this material to coaches. This is the material that we present to our players in Philadelphia. It is my hope that it will stimulate some ideas about the punt return.

Punt Return Personnel

We consider the punt return play to be the first play of our offensive series. Our defense has achieved a stop, providing a big psychological lift. We prepare to go on the attack. On the punt return play we always want to create at least one first down, as reflected in our goal of averaging 10 yards per punt return. By doing so, we take some of the pressure off our offense by presenting them with a shorter field to attack.

There are ways other than a great punt return to create those yards. We can pressure the punter into a poor punt and we can block punts. We can measure our success in these areas by calculating our opponents' net punt average, or the yards the opponent gains after all yards are tallied on the play. An NFL team who keeps the punting team to 33 or fewer net yards per punt on punt return plays is near the top of the NFL.

Before we can attempt to establish the first down on every play, however, we must do certain things to ensure that the punt return play is indeed the first play of the offensive series and not a play that puts our defense back on the field. Our first goal is to play sound football and avoid creating a negative play for our football team. The punt return unit's top priority is to make certain that after the play is completed, our offense takes the field. To achieve this goal, we do three things:

1. We account for any fake possibility by playing defense first.
2. We play with discipline at the line of scrimmage, in substitution, and around the punter to avoid penalties that lead to first downs.
3. We protect the football with the punt catch and return.

If we consistently do these three things, we will always start the series on offense and on a positive note.

We want to maintain an aggressive, attack-oriented mentality. The punt return is a great opportunity to create big plays. We can create big plays by flat-out being better than the punting team. We want to outplay our opponent both individually and collectively.

To win the play, we need to win the majority of the individual battles. Against a motivated, talented, and well-trained opponent, this is a difficult task. Coaches can give players the advantage they need to succeed by starting with the big picture and moving down through each detail. Later in this chapter we will discuss punt return and rush in more detail, but keep in mind that the effectiveness of the punt return unit is really the result of players' tenaciousness in every technique.

More than any other phase of the game, this phase is about effort. Most teams give a positive effort but rarely do they take it to the next level. Tenacious holdups and smart finishing blocks lead to big plays. Punt return units can develop a reputation for effort. They can also become known for pressuring punters into poor punts with aggressive force-the-punt rushes, and they can even become known for blocking punts.

The big picture of the punt return team can be broken down into the following core elements. The punt return team should embody these elements.

- *Knowledge.* The punt return unit thoroughly understands their job and their opponent.
- *Speed and effort.* Players on the punt return unit have the ability and willingness to expend the necessary effort to get in position to make plays.
- *Technique.* A player can beat a similarly talented and motivated player by understanding the geometry of the play, knowing the rules (what he is and is not allowed to do), and executing the proper technique.
- *Discipline.* Big plays are unnecessarily called back way too often. These penalties are a result of a lack of understanding or effort to do it the right way. Players can make any block if they know the technique and can do it at full speed.
- *Persistence.* Not every punt provides the opportunity for a block or big return. Players have to be willing to do it great every time out. Remember, "Nobody knows the day or hour."

The goal of the punt return unit is to create big plays in any way possible. Big punt return plays share certain characteristics that we strive to consistently achieve. The factors governing great punt returns are as follows:

- The returner demonstrates consistently good ball handling and decision making.

- The ball carrier uses aggressive north–south running.
- In coverage, the blockers are able to control the gunners and fullback (quick releasers).
- The unit has the ability to force returnable punts.
- The players are able to disrupt the coverage vertically or horizontally with good blocking.
- Everyone plays smart.

Players in the punt return unit need to play disciplined, intelligent football just like any other player in any other part of the game. Players can follow certain guidelines to accomplish that type of play. Disciplined and smart players on punt return

- know the rules;
- make sure the proper personnel are on the field;
- block above the waist, never in the back;
- know when to use their bodies instead of their hands to block;
- respect the punter (hitting or running into him is too costly);
- stay onside and know when the punting team will try to draw them offside;
- check teammates for onside alignments;
- get away from poison balls;
- ensure the defense of all fakes; and,
- make quality split-second judgments and decisions in various situations.

Punt Return Techniques

In order to outplay opponents, players need to out-execute them. There are only two ways to do so, and they go hand in hand. First, players must put forth their utmost effort. They must play incredibly hard because a worthy opponent will certainly do so as well. Second, players must play better than the opponent. The primary responsibility for making that happen falls on the coach. Only the coach can create schemes and techniques superior to the opponent's and teach them well so that players can execute them. The techniques in this chapter help our players do their job better than the opposing punting team.

Every block can be made. It is just a matter of knowing how to get it done and being willing to put forth relentless effort. We practice these techniques regularly at a high intensity. Players can get really good at these techniques if they have the desire.

A player can quickly, almost thoughtlessly, go through a checklist of points as he sets up for the play. This is the takeoff progression we use:

1. Set up in proper alignment.
2. Be aware of fake responsibility.
3. See the ball and takeoff key (center hitch, etc.).
4. Get a great start with the proper angles and body position. Push off the front foot.
5. Properly react to fakes when one occurs out of the blue.
6. Beat your man to the punch with a quick start. Change up the scheme to keep him off balance.
7. Execute effective and disciplined blocking techniques.

To carry out his assignment, the player should be prepared to find a way to block his man from the very start of the play. To block effectively, the player needs to be equipped with various tools. His coaches can teach him those tools, also called techniques. Blockers will encounter many different situations and obstacles to making blocks. We tell our guys that no two punt returns are ever exactly the same. Each play demands a different reaction. The following techniques are the tools players use to make that block.

Holdup

Players want to keep their men from releasing vertically into the punt coverage for as long as they can. The goal is to create as much vertical separation as possible between the coverage unit and the returner. By doing so, the blocking unit establishes free yards in which the ball carrier is running upfield against only air.

For the holdup technique, we teach players the following skills.

- With strong hands, fit into the block inside the opponent's framework. Work heavy over the player's outside number since most teams release outside in order to fan out on the field. Stay square and in front to close the gate on the opponent's release.
- Strike to gain control of the opponent's balance. Time the punch with the legs, hips, and torso as well as the hands to deliver a blow, usually on the second or third step.
- Keep your base up to control your balance. When the opponent responds, drop your weight and widen your base. Your hands should be above your head and your hips should be bent and low.
- Move your feet and work your hands to maintain the closed gate and to stick and stay in front of the opponent. This skill is about tenaciousness.

Trail and Harass

After the opponent releases, the player blocking the opponent wants to control the opponent's progress down the field. The player's next objective is to widen the opponent's route and slow him down. Widening the opponent off his desired path disrupts the opponent's spacing, creating horizontal seams in the coverage. By impeding the opponent's progress and slowing him down, the punt return unit creates vertical space for the ball carrier.

For the trail and harass technique, we teach players the following skills:

- Immediately widen the opponent's route with a hard shove as he releases across the line of scrimmage.
- Run slightly behind the opponent on his inside hip.
- Harass the opponent by pushing him on the side or knocking his arm off stride as he runs.
- Anticipate the angles that are being created and work to establish position to finish the block.

Counter Trail

The counter-trail technique is a changeup of the trail and harass technique. Show trail and harass to the side opposite of the intended return direction and the opponent will tend to overplay that way. At 15 to 20 yards from the returner, pull yourself across the opponent's body and work to fit to the return side.

Deep

The deep technique is a block directly in front of the returner. A designated dropper or a second returner we call our deep player carries out the block. The purpose of the deep technique is to establish a blocker directly in front of the ball carrier. This blocker accounts for the first cover man to pose a threat to the ball carrier. The deep player may end up blocking a player who was accounted for but who beat the initial blocker. The deep player may also end up blocking a cover man who was unaccounted for. This is the progression for the deep technique:

1. Fulfill your initial fake responsibility by clearing the punt before turning and running.
2. Sprint on an angle, chasing the punt to get in front of the returner.
3. Set up 10 to 15 yards in front of the ball carrier.
4. Set up on the run if the returner gets the ball before you get there.

5. Block the most dangerous man (MDM) whichever way he wants to go.

6. Know who is unblocked in the scheme, who the best coverers are, and who the vulnerable corner is.

7. Check for a quick releasing threat.

There are always punt coverage players who cannot be accounted for, especially if we choose to block some coverers with two blockers. This means we must decide which players we will leave unblocked. We can either pick out the less able guys or we can establish a technique in which we block the most dangerous players once the punt begins to play out. We use both methods, though not at the same time.

Backside Wall

The deep technique is one of our MDM methods. Another way to block the most dangerous coverage men is to sort out the faster players on the backside of directional returns. This is our backside wall technique.

We use the backside wall technique when we block two on three with our front blockers on the backside of a directional return. We assign two blockers on the backside of the return direction to block the most dangerous guard, tackle, and slot. The most dangerous guard, tackle, and slot are those who get out the fastest and pose the most immediate threat to the returner. The progression is as follows:

1. The backside inside player secures the fake and stays out of picks.

2. After the punt, he sprints directly at the returner to 15 yards in front of him.

3. He finds and blocks the most dangerous backside guard, tackle, and slot.

4. The backside outside player usually forces the punt with an aggressive rush.

5. He also finds the returner and sprints at him, chasing his partner, the inside blocker.

6. He finds and blocks the second MDM on the backside.

Finishes

To achieve a great finish, players must understand the coverage geometry. Talk to blockers about the big picture of the play. Punt coverers must take certain angles to get in position to make tackles. Although the angles become apparent once the return play begins to develop, they can be anticipated. Certainly the cover man must anticipate these angles, and if the cover man can see them, so can the blocker. When the blocker anticipates the angle, he can get into position in the cover man's path and set up the block. In effect, the block comes to him. No two return plays ever set up exactly the same way, however, so players must learn to anticipate the general speed and angles. This is the geometry of the play. If players understand the geometry, they can anticipate where to go to make the play. The players are in position to finish the block every time, almost as if they can read the cover man's mind.

No two finish situations are exactly the same. Players must be prepared to make sound decisions based on the situation. Each situation demands a slightly different approach to the finish depending on the best method to keep the cover man off the ball carrier. We work on these types of finish blocks:

- *Inside-hand fit and finish*. When in a great trail position 5 to 10 yards from the ball carrier, punch his inside number and then establish a two-hand fit. Keep your base up and climb.

- *Inside-hand side fit and finish*. When in a great trail position 5 to 10 yards from the ball carrier but unable to get your hand in front due to the cover man's body position, punch the cover man's shoulder-pad side to establish a two-hand fit in front of him inside his framework. Keep your base up and climb. Do not put your hand on his back.

- *Hip by finish*. When in a deeper trail position 2 to 6 yards from the ball carrier, put your hands up or through and work into the cover man with your hips and legs. Be sure to get your hands up or through. Use your hips to press the cover man, similar to a box-out in basketball. Be physical so that you do not get pushed into the returner.

- *Midpoint finish*. When the cover man is farther out in front of you, locate and run to the midpoint between him and the returner. Your goal is to cut him off at the pass. You must recognize when the ball carrier starts coming downfield and calculate his angle. Finish the block depending on the cover man's relationship to the ball carrier.

- *Wall finish*. We use the wall finish when we force a punt and work back into position for a late block. Take a picture of the return and the coverage threats. Establish an angle to get between the cover man and the ball carrier's anticipated angle. Block the cover man with the best technique for the situation.

- *Knockout finish*. The knockout finish happens when the stars are aligned perfectly. You know what to do. This is the big hit that draws oohs and aahs from the crowd. Go for the big hit when you are looking in the cover man's ear hole instead of his eyes and you can make legal contact.

- *Retrace and climb finish*. Your ability to finish blocks depends on opening up your vision. Learn to locate both the returner and your cover man at the same time. Once you see both players, it becomes obvious which path the cover man will take. You can see where the returner is and how fast he is going when he catches the punt. The tendency is to overshoot the cover man. Anticipate his fold, especially when he is 10 yards or more from the returner. Your goal is to stay between your man and the ball carrier's path. We call this retracing your steps and climbing your man.

All of these techniques for blocking players on the punt coverage team give the return players an edge. Each technique demands maximal effort and concentration. It is equally important for players not to get tunnel vision on technique and lose sight of the bigger defensive picture. Players must keep in mind that the punt return is essentially a defensive play. The opponent has possession of the ball and is certainly entitled to and capable of earning a first down on the play, so we must establish ourselves as a defensive unit first. We must never allow the opposition to successfully execute a fake against us.

Defending Against Punt Fakes

We defend against fakes in a variety of ways. The safest and most basic method to defend against fakes is to leave the defense on the field. This is what most teams call defense stay. Usually we set up the defense stay in the same manner as the basic defensive front and coverage. We can execute it from any personnel grouping that might be on the field on third down. The only substitution is the returner if he is not already out there. It is best to go with defense stay when a fake is more of a possibility, such as in short-yardage situations or certain areas of the field. You should also take into account the game situation. Be wary of fakes when you are playing with the lead.

However, if we want to create field position for our team, we cannot afford to keep our defense out there on every punt return. We need a well-trained, talented punt return team on the field. Although this unit is in an attack frame of mind, they must be prepared to defend against fakes. First, players need to know the situation (down and distance, field position, and so on) and recognize formation, alignment, and personnel variations. Second, players defend against fakes by focusing on their assigned run-and-pass defensive responsibilities. Punt teams do not run offensive plays as effectively as offensive units do, and players who pay attention to their assignments in this area and stay aware of the situation will fare well against fakes.

We always account for any possible fake on every play. The resources we commit to fake defense depend on the chances of getting a fake on that play. We have a set of man-to-man coverage assignments. The run assignments correspond to basic gap control.

Coverage assignments*

    Corners: Cover gunners

    Safeties: Cover slots

    Backer: Cover personal protector

    Ends: Contain rush (blitz, engage punter, and flair peel)

    Guards and tackles: Run defense and pursuit

To successfully set up a punt return, it is vital to block the quickest releasers in the punt coverage unit. In spread punt formations, which most teams use, the quickest releasers are usually the widest aligned players, commonly referred to as the gunners. They split out from the main protection group and have room to release with no punt protection responsibility. They are capable of getting in front of the returner very quickly, even before the ball arrives, forcing a fair catch. If the gunners are not blocked, they will stop most returns before they get started. Success takes great athletes as well as great technique. We block gunners with a variety of looks and techniques.

Single techniques are the techniques we use when assigning one blocker to a gunner. It is best to use these techniques with a favorable matchup since they free another blocker. Vise techniques assign two blockers to a gunner. Following each technique is an outline of the progressions.

Bump and Run

The bump and run is a one-on-one technique designed to slow the gunner's release and then wall him away from the returner. It is similar to the defensive back's press man technique.

Line of scrimmage progression

    1. Align on the gunner's inside number.

    2. Stay square and keep the gate closed. Do not allow free access.

    3. Maintain your base.

    4. Time your punch to the gunner's release.

    5. Do not lunge.

    6. Maintain hand contact on the gunner throughout the play if possible.

Line of scrimmage options

    1. Mirror

    2. Jam jump set

---

*The backer may handle slot or personal protector until the safety can pick it up from the vise alignment.

3. Fake jam and skate

4. Fade steps square

Downfield progression

1. Trail on or slightly behind the gunner's inside or outside hip according to his release.

2. Harass the gunner and maintain contact if you are fast enough to do so.

3. If the gunner clears you, run to the midpoint cutoff and push him past the returner.

4. At 15 to 20 yards, recognize the geometry of the return and decide which finishing technique to use.

Vise

The vise is a two-on-one technique. It requires a big resource commitment, so with this technique we must be sure to get the job done every time. We refer to the inside vise player as the safety and the outside vise player as the corner.

Line of scrimmage progression

1. Align on the gunner's near shoulder pad. There should be some space between the two vise players.

2. Align square to the gunner and crowd the line of scrimmage, being sure to stay onside.

3. Use a corner stance.

4. At the snap, execute the start step toward your side, keeping the inside foot down.

5. Play aggressively over the gunner's near shoulder pad.

6. Know where your help is. Your partner is your help man.

7. React with the mirror drill and jam the gunner aggressively.

Vise progression

1. Lock down the gunner at the line of scrimmage if possible.

2. Do not cross your feet.

3. Put your chest on the gunner and stay on the outside half.

4. The backside player closes the gap quickly and physically— piranha.

5. Fit hip to hip with your help man; have high hands, moving feet, and the gunner locked in the vise.

Downfield progression

1. If the gunner clears vertically, be physical with your last shot.
2. The opposite blocker works the mirror relationship off his man.
3. Mirror the gunner on the same angle as he is to your help man.
4. Attack the gunner aggressively if he clears. It doesn't matter whether he clears over the top or underneath your partner.
5. When you get cleared as a blocker, fold back into the same mirror position.
6. Any time your help man secures the block, peel inside and pick up the MDM.
7. Apply finishing skills at the top, between the gunner and the ball carrier.

Vise changeups (communicate any changeups presnap)

- Invite split—Widen the alignment to invite the split and lock down the gunner when he goes for it.
- Jump set—One side attacks the anticipated release side and takes it away; quick piranha from the other side.
- Cut off—On ladder, the first man runs by, forcing the stutter, and the second man nails him.
- Half vise—The corner plays down the middle and forces a flat release either way. Against an outside release, the half vise becomes a single technique and the safety peels immediately. Against an inside release, the corner funnels the gunner to the safety, who strikes him; they lock him down from there.
- Bail—Use the single technique to attempt to force the gunner outside. The safety checks for the fake and then works into position to cut off the vertically releasing gunner. If the corner has the gunner blocked, the safety peels inside for the MDM.

Peel

We use the peel technique on a double-team block to block the MDM on a punt return. When a vise player secures the gunner, the other vise player turns back in front of the returner. He works to a point 15 to 20 yards in front of the ball carrier. This is similar to the deep technique (page 46). The vise player picks up the MDM with a legal block.

Types of Protection

The punt return unit wants to rush the punter in order to block punts or pressure the punter into poor punts. Pressuring the punter by stressing his protection creates opportunities for positive plays. To stress the protection, players need to understand how the protection works. Each week, we install a scheme within the basic system to stress our opponent's punt team in some way. We do not want to go at their strengths; we want to stress them where they are most vulnerable in personnel or scheme. We break down the opponent's punting team, paying particular attention to these components of their punt protection:

- Formation
- Style (man, zone, combo)
- Calls
- Weakest protector
- Scheme weakness
- Snapper's ability and tendencies
- Punter's ability and tendencies
- Gameday adjustments

Punt protection has been evolving as long as football has been played, and this is especially true of the past 10 years or so. There are many variations on punt protection, but they fall into these general categories.

Man

Each punting team member is assigned a particular defender to block, usually with a pass off of any twist. Man protection is more communication oriented and less choreographed than zone protection. We attack man protection by beating weak blockers or by trying to create a split second of indecision as to whom to block.

Characteristics of man protection
- Wider splits
- Blockers point at opponents and call numbers
- Blockers communicate more and stay at the line of scrimmage longer
- Center and personal protector split on assigned men

Zone

Zone protection is area blocking. Each blocker is assigned the rusher or rushers in his designated area. It does not matter how they align or who moves where, the players block their area. We attack zone protection by overloading areas and gaps and disrupting the rushers' spacing. We also like to run them deep and back them into the punter's lap.

Characteristics of zone protection
- Tighter splits, especially in the A-gap
- Blockers don't point or look directly at opponents
- Blockers communicate less on the line of scrimmage
- Quicker snap
- Deeper sets

Combo

Combo is a combination of man and zone protection. Usually it consists of man protection on the personal protector's side and zone on the center's side. Attack combo protection by determining which side is man and which is zone and attacking them appropriately. You can also to try to get five rushers over to the man side against their four blockers and three against the zone side.

Punt Block Techniques

We rush the punter from six, seven, or eight box looks. Players may be trying to hold up, rush, force the punt, or pick for a teammate, but their mentality on the first two steps is the same: "I am going to block this punt." Players must never be caught flatfooted on the snap of the ball. The first two steps are quick and aggressive. If they make a mistake in protection, they need to be in position to make the block. Most punt blocks in the NFL are the result of a missed assignment by the punt team. Getoffs need to be quick. Players force the punt team to block them on every punt, which in turn helps the punt return unit hold up the punting team for big returns.

Players must have confidence in their ability to make successful blocks. Technique and knowledge of the punter's block point and getoff time are critical. Everyone must develop a mental clock of when to attempt the block and when to shift to an aggressive holdup. All of this occurs by the third step.

General principles guide the players in this unit to make sound split-second judgments. The coach can help by providing players with guidelines that assist players in situations that are not black and white (most situations in football). These are the principles that apply to punt blocks:

- Know your assignment.
- Know the punter's block spot.
- Know the punter's getoff time (mental clock).
- Know when fewer than 5 yards is needed for a first down; be ready for a hard count.
- Execute a great getoff. Key the back tip of the ball and the center. Do not be called for offsides.
- If you get blocked, then block your blocker. Don't let your blocker block two.
- When the punt is blocked, the first man scoops the ball and scores. The second man blocks the punter or the first player in a wrong-colored jersey.

Certain coaching points that apply to punt blocking should be taught and reinforced consistently:

- Crowd the ball (alert neutral zone). Ends check alignment.
- Keep weight on your front foot.
- Use the best start stance that you have.
- Key the back tip of the ball and the center's elbows and hips.
- Keep your pads down.
- Inside rushers don't jump to make block.
- Accelerate across the block spot.
- Extend your hands, arms, and body by your sixth step.
- Flatten over the block spot, extending your torso out and flat.
- Push off the last inside step to extend.
- Keep your lower arm straight; allow movement in your upper arm. The upper arm adjusts to the punter's foot.
- See the ball come off the punter's foot. Keep your eyes open, as if hitting a softball.
- Get a hand out in the block spot.
- See the ball hit your hand.
- Take the ball off the punter's foot.
- Block the ball like a volleyball block.
- Avoid contact with the punter (discipline).

These are the specific techniques we teach:

• *Speed* (figure 3.1). After a great getoff, rush straight at the man in front of you. Beat the blocker outside and over the top. Swipe with your hands. Keep your pads down. Bend to the block point and block the punt.

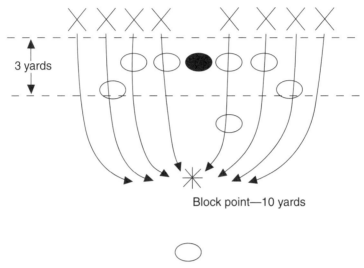

Figure 3.1 Speed rush.

• *Speed rip inside* (figure 3.2). Execute a great getoff. Take the first step straight ahead with the outside foot—sell the speed rush. Take the second step lateral inside the blocker. Club and rip inside the blocker. Keep your pads low. Block the punt.

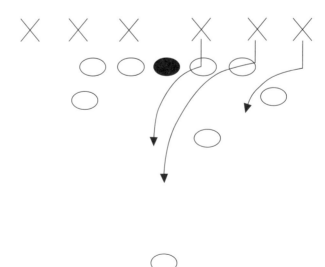

Figure 3.2 Speed rip.

- *Speed to power* (figure 3.3). After a great getoff, rush straight ahead at the man in front of you. Get your hands inside the blocker's chest and accelerate your feet to the block point. Run the blocker into the block point.

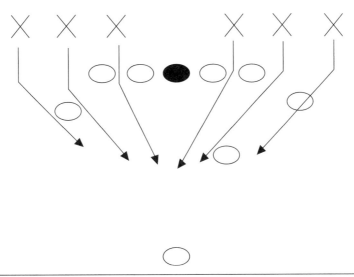

Figure 3.3   Speed to power.

- *Up and under* (figure 3.4). After a great getoff, rush hard upfield for two or three steps. Sell the outside speed rush. When your outside foot hits the ground (second or third step), hop inside of the blocker. Use your inside hand to club across the blocker. Accelerate to the block point and block the punt. Adjust the starting stance to get the proper steps.

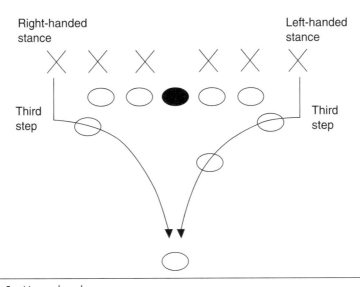

Figure 3.4   Up and under.

- *Ricochet* (figure 3.5). Execute a great getoff. The first man to go on a twist stunt uses the ricochet technique. Penetrate the gap, keep the pads low, and get to the blocker's hip (pick). When the blocker comes off, accelerate to the block point and block the punt.

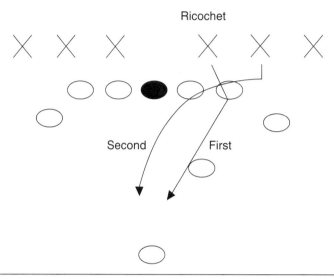

Figure 3.5 Ricochet.

- *Flash and go* (figure 3.6). Usually the flash and go is done out of a six or seven box holdup look. Use a great getoff. Step hard to the blocker and throw your hands at him as if it were a holdup. When he tries to release, accelerate by him with a rip move and block the punt.

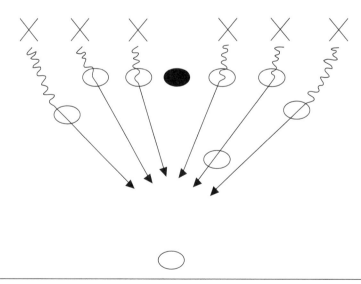

Figure 3.6 Flash and go.

Coaching the punt return team is challenging but fun. A punt return presents an opportunity to create a big play and gain valuable field position. The punt return is a defensive play that transitions into an offensive play when the ball is punted, so it entails diverse techniques. Developing these techniques is part of what makes coaching enjoyable. In the end, however, coaching the punt return is about getting players to play with tenacity. Superior effort combined with solid self-discipline creates success. Coach your guys to be great!

CHAPTER 4

© Dale Zanine/Icon SMI

KICKOFF RETURNS

DAVE UNGERER
University of Alabama

Special teams play is a part of football that I truly love. I am proud to represent the University of Alabama and all the great players and coaches I have worked with at Cal and Lehigh. We started a pretty good tradition of kickoff return the last few seasons. We had a lot of success during the 2003-2004 season, finishing fifth as a team. Our top returner, Lashon Ward, finished third in the nation. The two previous seasons we had one of the best returns in 1AA ball.

The formation we use is a little unusual in that we employ only a four-man front (figure 4.1). Most teams do not use the four-man front because of the threat of an onside kick. However, I don't believe that the four-man front is any more at risk from an onside kick than the five-man front. If the ball bounces funny or the player who should field the ball doesn't catch it cleanly, it wouldn't matter if you had a seven-man front. In my book, it is worth the risk to have two more blockers 10 yards behind the front four. These two blockers have better leverage, better blocking angles, and bigger bodies. The added depth means they won't be outrun. Of course, we practice the surprise onside each week. Early last season, one team tried to onside against us and we recovered at the 50-yard line, first and 10. No one else tried it for the rest of the year.

The kickoff team must stay in their lanes for as long as possible to cover the field and make the defending team play the entire field. The other key to a successful kickoff return is making the cover team cover the whole 53 1/3 yards. That is why we base our game plan on whether our opponent kicks off from the middle or from the hash. If they kick off from the middle, we return right or left. If they kick off from the hash mark, we run the return into the boundary or counter back to the field.

Return Philosophy

The primary objective of the kickoff return team is to gain as much field position as possible for the offense. We can accomplish this objective if our return team understands and applies certain principles. Great effort is a must. Each player must go all out to fulfill his role on the return team. Each player must know his assignment and be able to adjust that assignment depending on where the ball is kicked. Errors in judgment can be catastrophic. A clip or a bad decision by the returner can result in poor field position or a turnover. No block is unimportant. The block farthest from the point of attack may be the block that makes a big return possible.

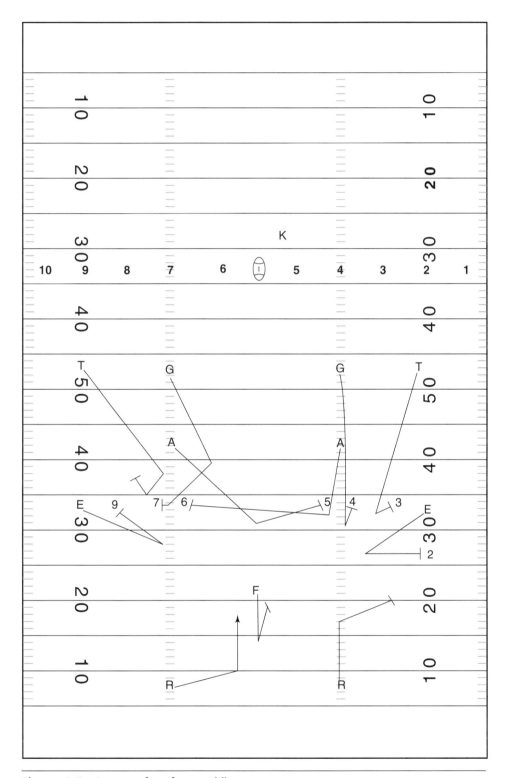

Figure 4.1 Four-man front for a middle return.

Keys to an Effective Kickoff Return

- Focus on turning the tide now.

- Make sure the play is sound from the middle of the field or the hash mark.

- Make the kicking team defend the whole field.

- Find a special player to be the returner.

- Prepare for special situations such as a sky kick (short kick; see figure 4.2), squib kick, or onside kick.

- Set a goal for the offensive drive to start at the 27-yard line.

We stress excellence in certain areas. First, we want to soften coverage. We want to keep the cover team honest and make them cover the entire field. We must be able to attack in all directions. The relationship between the ball, the blocker, and the cover team is crucial to any good return.

Second, we want to disguise all returns. As much as possible, we want to make the return and counter look the same. Notice the similarities between our trap right return (figure 4.3a) and our counter-right return (figure 4.3b). The similarities force the cover team to stay in their lanes longer and not collapse on the area where the ball is kicked. The coverage team must defend the entire field, thereby expanding the running lanes for the returner.

Finally, we want to force the ball upfield. Our returner must have confidence in the blockers. We must force the ball upfield and attack the coverage team. A good cover team can run down an east–west return.

This scheme has several advantages. First, it's easily fixable. We use a simple man-on-man return that helps us get helmet-on-helmet coverage for each of their cover players. A man-on-man scheme allows us to immediately find and fix any breakdown. Also, this man-to-man scheme is basic. It is good against all cover schemes and requires only a few small adjustments throughout the season. Any adjustments for containing great coverage players are simple. Another advantage of this scheme is it allows us to create easy double teams. We can make a simple call, "Double," and get our end to double with any of our frontline players. Finally, the scheme is time efficient. It gives us the ability to execute a play that we don't use very often with minimal practice time. We spend our time mastering the return rather than teaching adjustments.

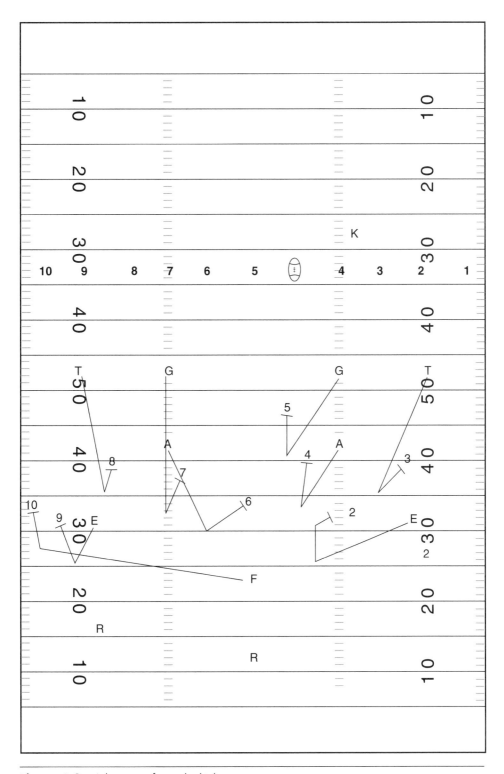

Figure 4.2 Adjustment for a sky kick.

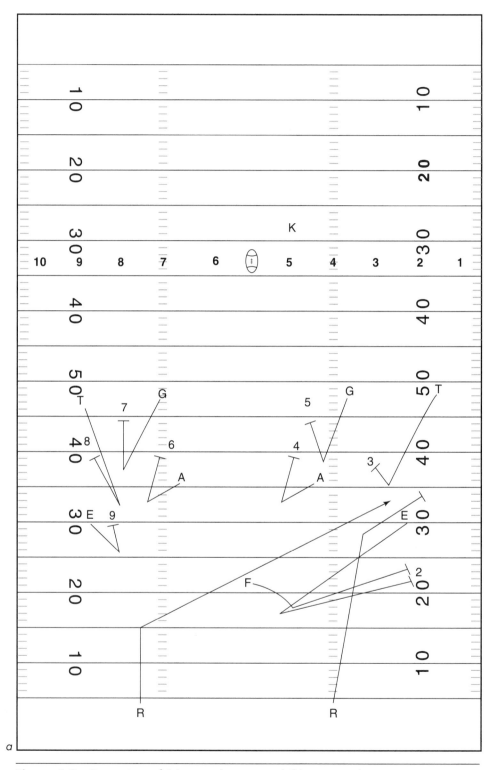

Figure 4.3 Comparison of *(a)* trap right return and *(b)* counter-right return.

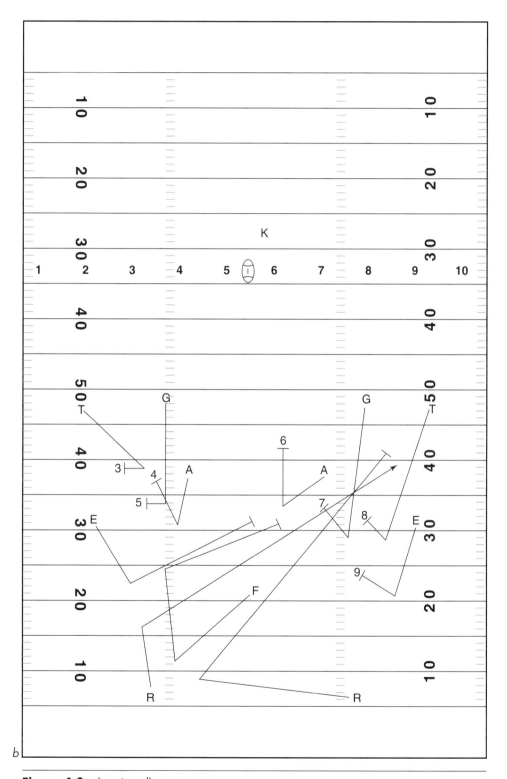

Figure 4.3 *(continued)*

Return Fundamentals

The front four line up 12 yards from the football. They must know where to move following a penalty. They must know where the ball becomes live. They must make all blocks above the waist. They must always see the kick and the flight of the ball.

Anticipate an onside kick if your team faces a 15-yard penalty on the kickoff. If the kicking team adjusts their formation for an onside kick, everyone must move accordingly. Figure 4.4 shows how we align when we are not sure if an onside kick is coming.

All players must remember to stay above the waist when blocking, always dropping to gain leverage. All blocks must be legal. Players must be constant in their alignments and never cheat on alignment. They must never align directly in front of a ball on a tee.

The frontline players must see the kick. They cannot leave until the ball has been kicked. As soon as the ball is kicked, the frontline players immediately focus on the returner. He is their eyes. Whatever direction the returner runs will tell the frontline players what angles they need in order to gain leverage on their man (snap key).

Each player sprints full speed. Each must run as fast as possible in order to get to the 30-yard line with at least a 5-yard cushion. Remember, the kicking team is running a flying 40.

When blocking, players must sustain their feet, maintaining their balance. All good blocks have punch, are at pad level, and include active, wide feet. Take the man square. Avoid angle blocks. Be the hammer, not the nail. Timing is crucial.

The frontline players allow flat power kicks to go through. For an onside kick, we never try to advance the kick; players just fall on the ball.

One man is in charge of calling who will handle the kickoff. He calls "Me-me-me," "You-you-you," or "Stay-stay-stay," depending on the kick. For the blockers to have a chance to be successful, the returner must be able to catch the ball while moving forward and execute the set and speed of this assignment.

The front four players must be strong blockers who can stop the feet of a cover player and keep him covered strong in the hips. They must be knee benders who can fit and finish. Players who don't have blocking leverage by alignment must gain it with their drops. They can create the best leverage by dropping to the ball side of the man to be blocked.

The backside A, backside guard, and backside tackle cannot get cross-faced. They must invite the speed move.

The returner must catch the ball with his shoulders square while moving slightly forward. This is the only way for him to get synchronized with the blocks. The ball must reach the strike zone at or just after the moment the blockers make contact.

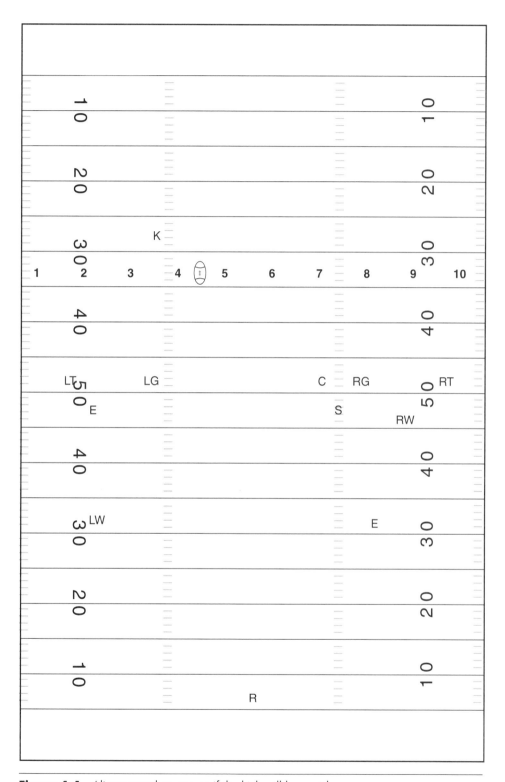

Figure 4.4 Alignment when unsure if the kick will be onside.

Every backfield player must understand that he is the eyes for the front six. Everybody must know what to do and why they are doing it. Everyone has someone else's back.

The Returner

The returner, or danger man, must catch all kickoffs. He fields all balls on the fly. He must not run a dropped ball out of the end zone. He must cover any kickoff into the end zone, because if the opponent recovers the ball in the end zone, it is a touchdown. If the returner brings the ball out of the end zone, he must not take it back into the end zone. If the returner downed it or the kicking team tackled him, the opponent would score a safety. In high school football, the kickoff may not be run out of the end zone.

The returner must keep a cool head while on the job. He must always be thinking. A bouncing kickoff that ricochets off the returner or one of his teammates into the end zone can be downed for a touchback. (The impetus that sent the kick into the end zone came from the kicker, even though it might have bounced off the returner or one of his teammates.)

The returner must know the kicker—where he puts the ball and his average distance, kick height, and hang time. He must be conscious of the wind. Is the wind with or against the kicker? How strong is the wind? The returner must know the coverage and how the kickoff team comes down the field.

Communication is the key to teamwork. Deep backs must talk to each other. The noncatching returner must be strong in his command of "Stay, stay, stay" if the ball is 4 yards deep in the end zone.

When fielding a ball that may go out of bounds, the returner always keeps his shoulders upfield. If he turns them, he should let the ball go out of bounds. He must be sure to chase the ball all the way out.

CHAPTER 5

© University of Iowa

EXTRA POINTS AND FIELD GOALS

LESTER ERB AND RONALD AIKEN
University of Iowa

Wins are difficult to come by. We concoct schemes, practice them all week, and maybe, just maybe, use them once during the game. We spend hours upon hours trying to get that extra edge or find that little tip that might win the game. In the process we sometimes end up neglecting the fundamentals of the game or taking for granted the special teams units that have the potential to win or lose the game.

Extra Point and Field Goal Protection

Extra point and field goal protection is often overlooked. It is easy to neglect it since extra points are supposed to be automatic, right? We have all won and lost games because of an extra point or because our opponent blocked a field goal attempt and returned for a touchdown. When this happens, we look at the film to see where the breakdown occurred and why it happened. Often technique is the reason. At the University of Iowa, our head coach, Kirk Ferentz, is adamant about coaching the finer points of every position and every unit. He is about paying attention to detail, using perfect technique, and trusting the fundamentals. He takes nothing for granted, not even extra point and field goal protection.

The placekick is crucial to success and often determines the final outcome of the game. We talk to our players about the importance of the FG–PAT (field goal–extra point) unit. We tell them that anytime we get within the 25-yard line, we have a great opportunity to score points. They should expect to score every time they take the field, but should not take it for granted. To be successful, the FG–PAT team must

- be disciplined in substitution;
- be disciplined in alignment and technique;
- have a great snap, hold, and kick;
- have confidence in our ability to execute the kick; and
- take pride in doing the job well.

This is how we coach the FG–PAT unit at Iowa. It isn't the only way to coach special teams, but it works well for us.

Huddle

The center sets the huddle 8 yards from the line of scrimmage with his back to the line of scrimmage. He always sets the huddle on the right hash mark unless the ball is on the right hash mark; in that case he sets the huddle to the left of the ball. In the huddle, the offensive linemen face the holder, standing tall. The wings and the ends are in front with their hands on their knees, looking up. Everyone in the huddle must give his full attention to the holder. The kicker is not in the huddle; he is finding his spot.

The holder is the quarterback of this unit. It is his huddle. He needs to take control! His first responsibility is counting to make sure there are 10 men in the huddle and the kicker is on the field. His second responsibility is making all calls inside the huddle. He will tell the unit whether the kick is normal or a fake, giving the call twice. For example, he might call, "Field goal on center snap, field goal on center snap," or, "Fake right on center snap, fake right on center snap." After the second call, the center leaves the huddle. The holder says, "Ready, break." The unit claps their hands on "break" and sprints to the line of scrimmage.

Alignments

The center leaves the huddle, approaches the ball, and gets into his stance as quickly as possible. The other players find their alignments based on the center. The guards take a three-point stance with the inside foot back and inside hand down. The guard to the center's right is in a left-handed stance. The guard's inside foot, the foot closest to the center, is directly behind the center's foot. Guards must be careful not to interlock with the center; that is a penalty. The guard's toes on the outside foot should be perpendicular to the center's foot. We want to create some vertical separation from the line of scrimmage. The guard must see the ball out of his peripheral vision.

Tackles base their alignments on the guards' alignment. Tackles take no more than a 6-inch split from the guards. Again, they use a three-point stance with the inside foot back and inside hand down. The tackle's toes on the outside foot should be perpendicular to the guard's foot. The tackle must see the ball out of his peripheral vision.

The ends take their alignments off the tackles. The ends align in a three-point stance with the inside foot back and inside hand down. The ends take no more than a 6-inch split from the tackles. The ends are different from the other interior linemen in that their outside foot is parallel to the tackle's outside foot. The ends should not create any more vertical separation from the line of scrimmage. Each end's helmet must be able to break the beltline of the center. If they do not break the beltline, there will not be enough men on the line of scrimmage. Ends also must see the ball out of their peripheral vision.

If you look at the FG–PAT unit's alignment from end to end, you should see a bow (figure 5.1). This bow actually widens the corners for the rush unit. If you line everyone from end to end on the same plane, the rush unit has better angle coming off the edges to the block point. You must have seven men on the line of scrimmage, so make sure that your front seven are aligned so that their helmets break the beltline of the center.

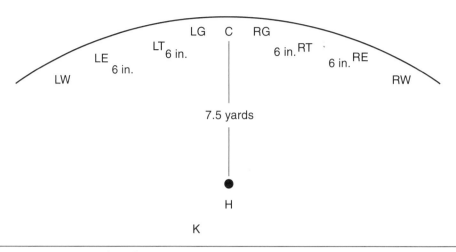

Figure 5.1 Bow at line of scrimmage.

Wings base their alignment on the ends. They use a two-point stance. Hands are on the knees, butt is down, and eyes are up. They align an arm's length off the end with the inside foot just behind the groin of the end. The wings face out at a 45-degree angle.

After breaking the huddle, the holder sets the spot for the kicker. The kicker should set his spot approximately 7 to 7 1/2 yards from the line of scrimmage. After the holder places his hand on the spot, the kicker can mark off his steps.

At Iowa, we use this alignment regardless of the hash mark the ball is placed on. If the ball is on either hash mark, you can use a tackle-over alignment (figure 5.2). On hash kicks the flight of the ball often shortens

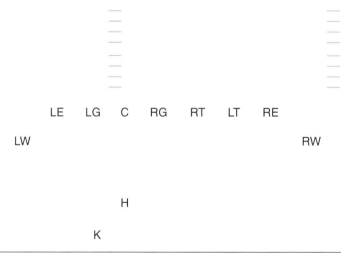

Figure 5.2 Tackle-over alignment.

the corner to the wide field. Some teams put the boundary-side tackle on the field. You only want to do this if you are kicking from the hash mark and are getting wide side rushes from the defense.

If you are kicking from the right hash mark, the wide side of the field is to the left. The right tackle aligns between the left tackle and the left end. The right tackle must now keep his outside foot parallel with the left tackle's outside foot. Again, his helmet should break the beltline of the center. If you were on the left hash mark, the left tackle would go to the right side.

The right tight end slides down beside the right guard. He can get some vertical separation from the line of scrimmage by moving his outside foot back to be perpendicular to the guard's outside foot. The techniques and footwork remain the same. By making these two simple personnel adjustments, you can take away the edge rushers' angle to the field.

Personnel Selection

When selecting personnel, we look for big bodies, especially for the interior line. At Iowa, we use offensive linemen as interior blockers, tackle to tackle. Because of our stance—inside foot back and inside hand down—we flip the line. Our left tackle on regular downs becomes our right tackle on FG–PAT tries and the left guard becomes the right guard, and vice versa. Since we flip our personnel, we do not need to teach the offensive linemen a different stance. They just assume their normal three-point stance.

We like to use tight ends in the end positions. First, they should have eligible numbers. They can be pass receivers on fakes or on fire calls, which we will discuss later. If a player with an eligible number is at the end position, the rush unit will have to account for him in coverage, taking one player out of the rush. However, having a tight end in the end position is not always possible. If you do not have enough tight ends who can hold up against a strong rush, or if injuries create a shortage of tight ends, do not hesitate to insert an extra offensive lineman. We have used tackles in the end positions on numerous occasions. A big drawback to using an extra offensive lineman at the end position, however, is that he is wearing an ineligible number and cannot be a pass receiver and cannot go downfield until the ball is kicked.

Wing positions are usually manned by fullbacks or tight ends. You want bigger guys who are mentally and physically strong. For one thing, most of the time wings block defensive backs coming off the edge. The rush unit has a running start coming off the edge and some good collisions happen between wings and edge rushers. Furthermore, wings often end up blocking two men. Wings must be willing to sacrifice their body because they are definitely going to take some shots.

The three most important members of the FG–PAT unit are the center, the holder, and the kicker. If you cannot snap the ball, hold the ball, or kick the ball, you might as well go for it! The center has to be an excellent short snapper. First and foremost, he must be able to get the ball back to the holder. Size is secondary, although of course a 185-pound wide receiver or defensive back is not a good idea as he would more than likely weaken the interior protection. We would all like a 300-pounder to be our best short snapper, but we do not usually have that luxury. The past three seasons here at Iowa we have had a 235-pound outside linebacker snapping field goals for us.

A good holder is vital to a good FG–PAT unit. We look for certain characteristics. First, the holder should be a skilled athlete. He must have soft hands, and he must be able to field all snaps cleanly. If the holder is double catching or is unable to handle bad snaps, the kicker will never be able to develop timing or confidence. A holder should be able to erase any minor mistake made by the center. He should be able to pick low balls like a shortstop and handle high balls like a wide receiver.

Second, the holder must have quick hands. After he catches the ball, he must put it on the spot quickly and accurately. He must also be able to find the laces and spin them away from the kicker in a fraction of a second.

Third, the holder should be able to throw the ball. Although this skill is not imperative, it opens up a variety of opportunities for fakes. It also helps on bad snaps when the holder makes a fire call.

Most importantly, the kicker must trust the holder. Ideally we want the punter to be the holder. The punter and kicker usually have a good working relationship. They spend a great deal of time doing repetitions together. They develop confidence and timing.

Quarterbacks, wide receivers, and punters are skilled athletes who handle the ball on every snap. Those positions are a good place to start when looking for a holder.

Obviously, the kicker will be the player who can kick the ball through the uprights most consistently. When we recruit kickers, however, we also look for athletes who have mental toughness. We want athletes who played other positions in high school, such as quarterback, defensive back, or wide receiver. For example, one of our kickers was Nate Kaeding, winner of the 2002 Lou Groza award. He was a three-sport athlete in high school. He started for the football team, the basketball team, and the soccer team. In his senior year, he won a state championship in all three sports. That is an amazing statistic. In fact, he kicked the game-winning goal in overtime to win the state championship for the soccer team. Nate is 6 feet tall and maybe 180 pounds, but if he were 220 pounds he would be playing middle linebacker. He is solid mentally and thrives on pressure.

Blocking Assignments

As mentioned before, the three most important members of the unit are the center, the holder, and the kicker. Their efficiency determines the protection unit's success.

We talk to the center, holder, and kicker about getting the kick away in less than 1.3 seconds from the time the center begins the snap until the kicker's foot hits the ball. You can survive up to about 1.35 seconds, but even then you run the risk of having a kicked blocked from the edge. We time every kick from preseason camp until the last game of the season, both on the field and from videotape. Holders and kickers are responsible for charting their times from practice tape. This gets them to watch tape and increases awareness of the importance of handling the ball.

FG–PAT protection is gap protection. Instruct players that they are blocking an area, not a man. Breakdowns occur when a blocker buries his head or blocks a man and allows someone to run through his gap. Emphasize keeping pads low, eyes up, and shoulders parallel to the line of scrimmage. In FG–PAT protection, the interior linemen never want to move their outside foot. The outside foot should stay in place, preventing them from widening the outside gap. Finally, players sprint to cover on a field goal after the ball is kicked. If the ball does not leave the playing field, it can be returned.

The center's responsibility is to throw a strike to the holder on every snap. After the holder calls "Set," the center can snap the ball at any time. Snappers tend to get into the habit of snapping the ball at the same time after every call. Coach them to vary the time between the set call and the snap. Most rush units study the snapper's rhythm to get a jump on the snap.

After the snap, the center must quickly get his head up and get a hand into each A-gap. The guards' initial steps allow the center to sit back on the guards' thigh pads. This should secure the A-gaps. Once the ball is kicked, the center covers downfield.

The guard's initial footwork is crucial to helping the center in protection. In the alignment, the guard's inside foot should be directly behind the center's adjacent foot. On the snap, the guard takes a quick punch step behind the center, no more than 6 inches. The foot should be on the ground at a 45-degree angle with the weight on the inside of the foot. The inside step should brace the center's near hip so he can sit back on the guards' thigh pads. The outside foot should not move. Keeping his pads parallel to the line of scrimmage, the guard wants to hit on the rise through his area. The guard's inside hand helps secure the A-gap and his outside hand aids the tackle in the B-gap. Once the ball is kicked, guards cover downfield.

The tackle's initial footwork is exactly the same as the guard's. On the snap, tackles take a quick punch step inside, no more than 6 inches. The inside foot ends up at a 45-degree angle with the weight on the inside of the foot. The outside foot stays in place. The tackle should brace the guard's outside leg while punching up on the rise through his area. His shoulders must be square to the line of scrimmage. His inside hand secures the B-gap, and his outside hand helps the end in the C-gap. Once the ball is kicked, tackles cover downfield.

The end's footwork is exactly the same as that of the guard and tackle. On the snap, ends take a quick punch step inside, no more than 6 inches. The inside foot ends up at a 45-degree angle with the weight on the inside of the foot. The outside foot stays in place. The end braces the tackle's outside leg while hitting up on the rise through his area. The inside hand secures the C-gap and the outside hand helps the wing secure the D-gap. Once the ball is kicked, ends cover downfield.

By alignment, the wing should be able to protect the D-gap. He will have some help from the end, but he is responsible for that gap. He may have to double bump the outside rusher. Keeping his inside foot in place, the wing punches his inside hand up through the D-gap, stiff arming any D-gap threat. He should keep his eyes on any outside rusher, timing the outside rusher's rush and getting his outside hand on the outside rusher's hip. He does not need to get much of the edge rusher, but needs to slow him down or redirect him. He should not move the inside foot or give up the D-gap. He must protect inside out. Wings cover downfield once the ball is kicked. In coverage, wings are contain players.

After breaking the huddle, the holder aligns on the spot picked by the kicker. He then double-checks to make sure 11 men are on the field. The holder waits until the kicker gives him the ready signal. Once the holder gets the ready signal, he checks to make sure the front is set and that there is no offensive movement. When the kicker is ready and the unit is set, the holder says, "Ready," and shows his right hand (or left hand for a left-handed kicker) to the center. The center can then snap the ball at his discretion. The unit moves on the snap of the ball, which is why the interior linemen must be able to see the ball in their peripheral vision. After the ball is kicked, the holder becomes a safety to the right in coverage.

The kicker marks his spot. When the holder places his hand on the spot, the kicker marks off his steps. Once he is set, the kicker nods at the holder to indicate he is ready to kick the ball. He becomes a safety to the left side in coverage.

Fire Call

Unfortunately, kicking a field goal or extra point is not automatic. Eventually the center is going to make a bad snap or the holder is going to mishandle a good one. In any case, having a fire call in your arsenal can get you out of a tough situation. In the event of a bad snap, or a snap that the holder cannot place on the spot in time for the kicker to kick the ball, the holder makes a fire call (figure 5.3). The holder repeats this call loudly several times.

When the holder makes the fire call, the ends and wings run mirroring routes on both sides. Wings release and run into the flat about 3 yards deep. On an extra point, they get into the end zone. On a field goal, they want to get deep enough to ensure a first down if they are thrown the ball. Ends run corner routes, aiming for the back pylon of the end zone on an extra point and for a spot on the sidelines about 12 to 15 yards deep on a field goal. They must make sure they get first-down yardage.

The holder or kicker, whoever picks up the ball, tucks the ball away and sprints out to the most convenient side. This is a run first, pass second option. The ball carrier should be thinking about getting the first down or getting into the end zone, depending on the position of the ball. Players should be aware of the yardage they need to get a first down. If the team needs 2 yards to a first down, they need to be sure to get 2 yards. No one needs a holder throwing an incomplete pass to a covered end 15 yards downfield when the flat route is open 3 yards downfield.

When the holder makes a fire call, the offensive linemen cannot go downfield. They must stay on the line of scrimmage and pass-block any man in their zones. Furthermore, any player wearing an ineligible number cannot go downfield. If you have substituted an extra offensive lineman at the end position, coach him to not release on a fire call.

We install a fire call early in preseason camp. Bad snaps and mishandled snaps are going to happen, so when they do occur, play them out as fire calls and instruct the entire unit. We practice one or two fire calls every

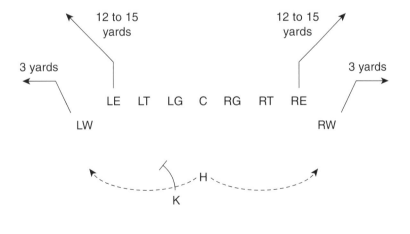

Figure 5.3 Fire call.

week during game preparation if one does not happen naturally. Take the time to coach it. With luck you will never need it, but when the situation comes up, you want players to react quickly and confidently.

Coaching Responsibilities

At Iowa, each special team has a coordinator. Since we designate the FG–PAT unit as an offensive special team, the offensive staff takes on the coaching responsibilities for the unit. The tight ends coach is the coordinator of the FG–PAT unit. As the coordinator, he breaks down opponent film, hands out scouting reports, and handles all game planning. He is responsible for reviewing the game film and grading all plays. He is also responsible for the ends during practice and games.

The offensive line coach is responsible for the interior protection unit, from tackle to tackle. He is responsible for teaching technique and responsibilities to those positions. The running backs coach handles the wings, and the quarterbacks coach handles the holders. The wide receivers coach is responsible for the timing of each repetition and for the snapper and kicker.

As you can see, all our offensive coaches are involved in this unit. Since responsibilities are delegated among the staff, each player receives constant feedback. This makes the unit more detailed in not only assignments but also technique. Moreover, for one coach to see what all 11 men are doing is almost impossible. You create a better learning environment by getting everyone involved.

Practice Breakdown

The first day of preseason camp we install the FG–PAT protection during practice. We use a five-minute segment, splitting up according to coaching responsibilities. We divide into three stations and walk through alignments, assignments, and techniques. The offensive line coach takes the interior protection and talks through the techniques and assignments. The tight ends coach and running backs coach do the same with the ends and the wings, while the kickers, holders, and snappers work on operation and cadence. If we come out of the first day knowing where to line up and what our assignments are, we have improved.

At the second practice, we again break down into the three stations. It is still a five-minute segment, but now we speed up the tempo. We begin to emphasize technique while detailing alignment and assignment. Although we increase tempo, we are more interested in doing it the correct way than getting a lot of repetitions.

Our offensive line coach puts a group of six reserves on defense as the rush unit. These six reserves rush a gap so the protection unit can work on technique. We emphasize footwork, hand placement, and parallel shoulders. After the protection unit gets three rushes, the next group rotates through (figure 5.4).

Tight ends and wings work a three-on-two drill (figure 5.5) in which three rushers rush the C-gap, the D-gap, and the edge. This drill lets the wings practice the double-bump technique off the edge. This drill does not have to be full speed. Half speed is plenty. You are not looking for collisions; you want to instill good technique and confidence.

The snappers, holders, and kickers are still working operational mechanics. The holder learns all of his responsibilities during this drill. You need a smooth operation, and here is where you lay the foundation. The kicker does not kick any balls. The holder goes through his checklist and makes his calls. After the ready call, the ball is snapped and the kicker approaches the ball but does not kick it.

On the third day of practice, we put the unit together and do the full operation, taking live kicks versus air. We huddle on the first one but repeat three times from the line of scrimmage. After three repetitions, we rotate groups.

In camp, every day starting with the fourth practice we go against the defensive rush unit. Each practice we do a three- to five-minute segment of FG–PAT unit versus FG–PAT rush. We do this live off the edges during regular practice days, but the interior rush unit only steps to their gaps

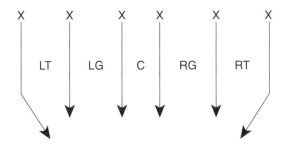

Figure 5.4 Interior protection drill.

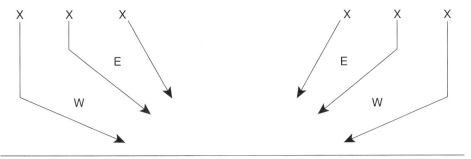

Figure 5.5 Three-on-two drill for ends and wings.

and gets their hands up. We do an all-out live rush on some scrimmage days. Once the game-week preparations begin, we work against a scout team. The scout team should be similar to what you expect to see from the opponent.

At Iowa, we practice FG–PAT protection every day. Tuesday through Thursday practices have a three- to five-minute segment for FG–PAT. You should be able to get 8 to 10 repetitions. On Fridays we walk through a substitution drill. That is our practice schedule for the week.

Special Situations

You should practice some special situations throughout camp and the season. The first scenario occurs at the end of the half or the game. It is fourth down and the offense has no time-outs and cannot stop the clock. The FG–PAT team runs on the field and with no huddle they must snap the ball before time runs out. We practice this at the end of a two-minute drill. When the holder is running on the field, he uses a towel to signal a desperation kick. Everyone on the field knows the signal so we do not have any substitution errors.

In the second situation, the defense tries to freeze the kicker. We use the same two-minute drill scenario but when the kicker prepares to give the ready signal to the holder, we have the defense call time-out to ice the kicker.

In the third situation, we are kicking from the right hash on the 1- or 2-yard line and we want to take a delay of game penalty to create a better angle for the kicker. The defense can always decline, but it is worth a shot. To practice this, we simulate taking a penalty to get the ball backed up.

Finally, each week we practice a field goal fake. We plan a fake based on the opponent's fronts or tendencies. A simple but effective fake is a dive over the right side. The holder places the ball on the ground and then runs for the tackle's outside leg. Run this play away from the block side or versus a middle block. The front-side blockers block the inside gap while the backside blockers reach the play side and then hinge. The kicker follows through his kick and looks for any penetration to the backside. The play-side wing wants to make sure no penetration comes through the D-gap (see figure 5.6).

Another fake is an all-purpose pass. The holder wants to run this play against a team that likes to block off the edge. The holder places the ball on the ground and then reverse-pivots out the right side. As with the fire call, the right wing is in the flat and the right tight end runs a corner route. The backside, however, is different. The left tight end runs a shallow drag route no deeper than 5 yards. He looks to get in a viable pass relationship with the holder. The left wing runs a deeper drag route and sits underneath the near upright. He is a safety valve in case the holder has to pull up or throw a desperation pass.

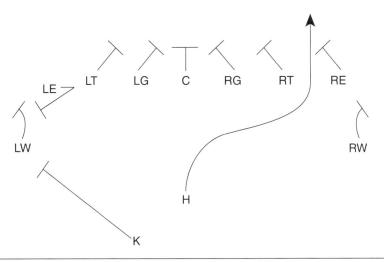

Figure 5.6 Field goal fake and run.

The holder has the option to run first, pass second. He should read from corner to flat to backside to dragging. If he gets run into a contain side, the flat should open quickly. The kicker follows through the kick and then looks for any backside chasers.

FG–PAT may not be the most glamorous or most difficult unit in football, but do not neglect its importance. Every time you send the kicker on the field, you could win or lose points. Hopefully you win more games kicking field goals than you lose getting field goals blocked. Kicking four field goals for the win may not be what the fans want, but a win is a win, and wins are hard to come by.

Extra Point and Field Goal Blocks

Special teams play has always been important to coaches. If you believe that special teams are an equal partner with offense and defense, then you agree that the kicking game requires at least as much practice as the other two areas. It does seem that for some team staff the extra-point block and the field goal block are often an afterthought. That is not the case at the University of Iowa.

Extra point and field goal attempts are two facets of the game that can dictate the game's outcome. Our philosophy, "The next play is the most important play," takes on special meaning when it comes to extra-point block and field goal block teams. No matter what big play just occurred or how the opponent scored, we must rise to the occasion and make the next play a big one. Getting a block or creating enough pressure to cause a shank on the extra point or field goal attempt can make a drastic difference in the outcome of a game.

I have had the opportunity in the last few years to oversee the extra point and field goal block segment of our special teams along with the defensive line. Most teams are extremely lax when attempting to block an extra point or field goal. Our approach is to line up and play the extra point or field goal block like a usual down on defense: Defend the goal line and don't give up any points. When attempting to block a field goal, we want to get off the field and deny our opponent the opportunity to score. Also, if the opportunity presents itself, we want to score. We cannot take that extra point or field goal for granted. We must bust our butt to create another opportunity to win the game. We must believe that we will win the game with defense!

We do not want to be caught unprepared to defend an unusual formation. To assist defensive players in making the switch to special teams, we help prepare them mentally.

Mental Preparation

Mental preparation for the FG–PAT block team begins with some strong dos and don'ts. First are the don'ts:

- Don't be offside.
- Don't rough the kicker.
- Don't have 12 men on the field.
- Don't let your mind wander. Be ready for the fake at all times.

Here are the dos for the FG–PAT block:

- Do move with the movement of the ball, not the sound of the call.
- Do play hardest on this play.
- Do use the proper angle and block point.
- When an extra point or field goal is blocked behind the line of scrimmage, do think offense.
- Do pick up the ball and run.
- Do be ready for the swinging gate. Shift to regular offense or any other type of fake.

Field goal and extra point defense must be prepared for certain situations. The extra point or field goal team may come out and line up in an offensive formation to run a play. They may shift to an unusual formation to run a play. Or they may substitute an unexpected player into the lineup.

Along with being alert for different alignments, you must also know the rules of extra point and field goal play. If the extra point is blocked and the ball is behind the line of scrimmage, you may advance it. The kicking team may also advance it if they regain possession. If a field goal is blocked behind the line of scrimmage, you may advance the ball. If the field goal is blocked and does not cross the line of scrimmage, either team may advance it.

If an attempted field goal is kicked from outside the 20-yard line and misses, the defense receives the ball at the line of scrimmage, so don't pick up the ball and return it.

This is an abbreviated list of the rules. Make sure your players know all the rules and how to apply them. If your players are prepared, they can execute quickly and efficiently.

Teaching and Implementing the Plan

For extra point and field goal blocking to bear fruit, you must break down the plan and communicate it clearly to the athletes at each position. When implementing a block, I like to divide the team into four groups. The defensive line works on alignment, takeoff, assignment, and technique. The coverage players work the fakes that the opponent has shown and they work on alignment and coverage. The edge blockers or second-level blockers work on the outside blocker's steps when going to block the point. We also study the look our opponents have shown in the previous weeks. Have the scout players give you the look of your opponent. The outside linebackers work with the blockers on alignment, shuffle, and scoop.

The following examples show our alignment and technique for our blocks, edge and safe, and swinging gate alignment. The extra point and field goal teams do not huddle, which allows us to look at the offense and make adjustments. Our Mike linebacker gets the signal from the sideline and makes the call.

Block R–L Block R–L (figure 5.7) is an overload to one side with pressure coming from the edge and over the offensive guard and tackle. One side of the defensive front is the block side and the other the backside.

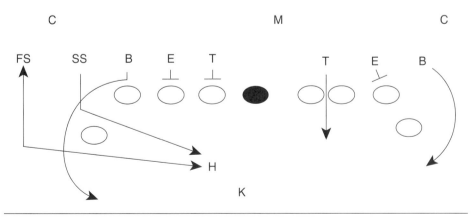

Figure 5.7 Block R–L.

The overload occurs when the strong safety and free safety (the best block personnel) line up to the block side. Our edge blockers, strong safety, or free safety can align in this position on the line of scrimmage or stem to the alignment.

Block-side tackle: Align head-up on the offensive guard, using a three-point stance with the inside foot back; execute four steps and get the hands up.

Backside tackle: Align at the B-gap away from the block side; attack the gap and get upfield.

Block-side end: Align head-up on the offensive tackle, using a three-point stance with the inside foot back; knock the offensive tackle back four steps and get the hands up.

Backside end: Align on the inside eye of the tight end, with the outside foot back; go man-to-man on the tight end.

Block-side linebacker: Align head-up on the tight end; attack the tight end, turning his shoulders inside toward the ball; shuffle outside and upfield; be prepared to scoop the ball and run if blocked; contain all fakes.

Backside linebacker: Align on the outside eye of the tight end; shuffle outside and upfield; be prepared to scoop the ball and run if blocked; contain all fakes.

Middle linebacker: Align over the center; go man-to-man on the block-side tight end; stem over the offensive guard when the kicking team is ready.

Strong safety: Align on the nose on the tight end's outside hip, using a three-point stance with the outside hand down and outside foot back; go to the block point 3 yards in front of holder, thumbs together and arms extended at block point.

Free safety: Align on the nose on the wing's outside hip; go to the block point 3 1/2 yards in front of holder, thumbs together and arms extended at the block point.

Corners: Go man-to-man on the wings.

Each defensive player must adhere to his specific responsibilities for the block to have a chance. Tackles, for instance, must exert enough push and get their hands up. Edge blockers must be tight off the edge and go to the block point.

The outside blocker drill (figure 5.8) teaches the outside rushers the proper takeoff and block angle. In this drill half the line lines up with the holder and kicker. The holder and kicker go through the normal kicking procedure. The blockers work on taking off with the ball movement and

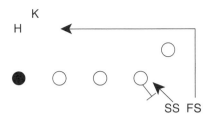

Figure 5.8 Outside blocker drill.

going to the block point. They use a three-point stance with the outside foot back. They key the ball out of the corner of their eye for takeoff. They turn the corner, flatten, and go to the block point.

The coach stands behind the blocker and tells him which player to let through. This way one blocker comes through free so we don't have a collision. When the rusher comes free, he should go to the block point with his eyes on the ball, thumbs together, and arms extended, and run through. Line up the dots to get the correct alignment for the guard and tackle. Align the center to snap the ball.

The outside linebacker drill (figure 5.9) teaches linebackers to scoop and score or contain on fakes. Both blockers align over (extra linebacker). They execute the collision and shuffle outside to execute their assignments. The coach flips the ball outside as if the ball were blocked. Players scoop the ball and run 10 yards, simulating scoring.

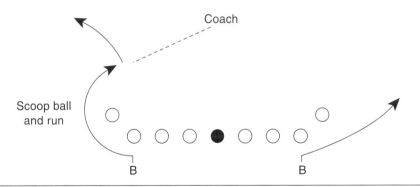

Figure 5.9 Outside linebacker drill.

The cover people drill (figure 5.10) teaches all players involved in coverage—specifically Mike and the corners—how to deal with possible fakes. Align the dots in the guard and tackle position with players in the tight end and wing positions to run routes. The coach stands on the defensive side of the ball and tells defensive players what routes to run. Defensive players are in man-to-man coverage.

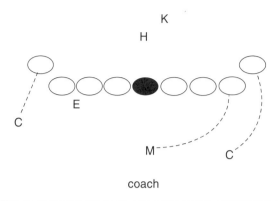

Figure 5.10 Cover people drill, M-C-C-C.

Jump Block Jump block will be used when the kicker has a tendency to kick the ball low or if the offensive line is soft up the middle in the protection. This information is gained by watching previous games of your opponent.

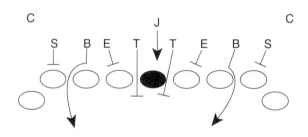

Figure 5.11 Jump block.

Blockers: Attack the offensive tackle and occupy him so he cannot attack the jumper, then work upfield for contain.

Jumper: Line up in the path of the ball; time the jump so that you can catch the ball coming off the ground.

Tackles: Attack the inside shoulder of the offensive guard; slide to the A-gap.

Ends: Attack the crook of the offensive guard's neck and take him back to the holder.

Safety: Cover the tight end man-to-man.

Corner: Cover the wing man-to-man.

The tackles and ends drill (figure 5.12) teaches tackles and ends to knock back the line of scrimmage and get their hands up. It also teaches the defensive tackle to penetrate and go for the block if the center attacks

Figure 5.12 Tackles and ends drill.

the jumper. Align tackles and ends on the offensive line and let them work on pushing back the line of scrimmage.

The jumper drill (figure 5.13) helps the jumper perfect his steps and timing. The jumper practices walking off steps from the ball so he will jump into the line of scrimmage. He lines up with a center holder and kicker, who go through their normal kicking procedure. When the ball is snapped, the jumper jumps to the block point.

Figure 5.13 Jumper drill.

The cover people drill for the corners and safeties (figure 5.14) teaches all coverage players how to deal with possible fakes. Align the dots in the guard and tackle positions with players in the tight end and wing positions to run routes. The coach stands on the defensive side of the ball and tells defensive players what routes to run. Defensive players are in man-to-man coverage.

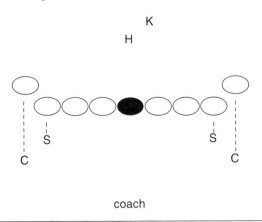

Figure 5.14 Cover people drill, C-S-SS-S.

Extra Point or Field Goal Safe   Situations when an opponent's field goal attempt is not as crucial to the final outcome as a first down or touchdown might be, dictate whether or not heavy pressure is placed on the kicker (safe). In these situations, you must put a little pressure on the kicker and be in position in case he misses or they fake the extra point or field goal. We refer to this as our safe block (figure 5.15).

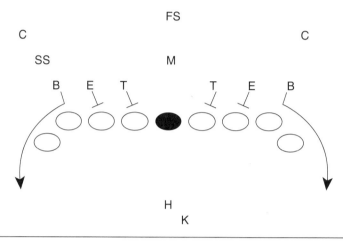

Figure 5.15   Safe block.

Tackles: Align on the offensive guard's outside shoulder.

Ends: Align on the offensive tackle's outside shoulder.

Outside linebacker: Align on the tight end's outside shoulder.

Middle linebacker: Align head-up on the center; stem to cover the tight end to your left, man-to-man.

Strong safety: Align head-up on the tight end to your right; cover the tight end man-to-man.

Corners: Align on the wing's outside eye; cover man-to-man on the wing.

Free safety: Align 8 yards off the line of scrimmage; be alert for fakes.

Defensive Alignment Versus Gate Formation   Some teams will align in unusual formation so you must be prepared for all trick plays and formations. Give your players a cover down rule that they can apply.

Right outside linebacker: Align on the end's outside eye on the line of scrimmage; contain all runs; against a pass, cover the tight end man-to-man.

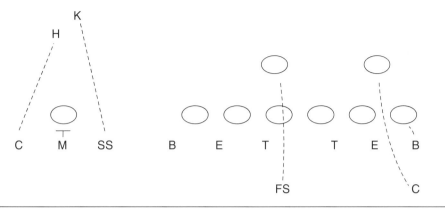

Figure 5.16 Alignment versus gate formation.

Left outside linebacker: Align on the outside eye of the last man on the line of scrimmage; keep your eyes on the ball; be alert for lateral to the wing; pick off any pass attempt.

Ends: Align on the tackle's outside shoulder; control your gap.

Tackles: Align on the guard's outside shoulder; control your gap.

Middle linebacker: Align head-up over the ball; cover the center man-to-man versus pass and run; after the gate shifts back to kicking formation, give the block call to the defense.

Left corner: Align on the line of scrimmage if the ball is snapped; blitz and engage the holder man-to-man.

Strong safety: Align off the line of scrimmage if the ball is snapped; take the kicker man-to-man.

Right corner: Align off the line of scrimmage in position to cover the right wing; if the ball is snapped, play the wing man-to-man.

Free safety: Align off the line of scrimmage in position to cover the left wing; if the ball is snapped, play the wing man-to-man.

Success in the offensive and defensive games depends on the flawless execution of each squad member's responsibilities, and the same principle applies to special teams. The bottom line is this—make something good happen!

When considering the appropriate action, obviously you must take into account such items as time, score, and possible momentum shifts. Once the decision is made to attempt a block, however, there is no substitute for adequate planning. Luck may sometimes account for the good things that happen in football games but, more often than not, it is the planning and practice that result in spectacular game-winning plays.

CHAPTER 6

© Human Kinetics

TWO-POINT CONVERSIONS

URBAN MEYER

University of Utah

I have had the opportunity to work with some of the most successful coaches in college football history. Every aspect of our program reflects my experiences working with these great coaches.

The one trait these coaches share is the belief that the team that is best prepared and most invested will win. This is reflected in their tireless, detailed dedication to getting their teams in position to succeed. This belief is the foundation of our program at Utah. I have yet to be involved in a game in which the best prepared and most invested team lost.

Serving on the staffs of Earle Bruce (Ohio State and Colorado State), Sonny Lubick (Colorado State), Lou Holtz (Notre Dame), and Bob Davie (Notre Dame) has provided me with time-tested methods for success, which I share here.

Plan to Win

We have developed a plan to win that is the basis for every decision we make within the program. Decisions about recruiting and personnel, staff hiring and evaluations, game planning, and game management are all kept in line with our plan to win.

The first element of our plan to win is playing great defense. This means hiring a great staff, making strong recruiting decisions, and managing the game properly. Proper game management means not placing our defense in bad situations.

The second element is winning the turnover battle. We place a premium on teaching ball security. Through our play calls, reads, and progression, we try to not put the quarterback in a turnover situation.

The third element is scoring in the red zone. We practice in this area of the field more than many teams. On average, a team is in the red zone only four times per game. However, defensive stops and offensive scores in this area can result in huge momentum swings. On offense, you want to score touchdowns on least three out of four trips in the red zone. When you play a ball-control game, you must score on every opportunity in the red zone. On defense, you do not want to give up any points, but you at least want to hold the offense to a field goal.

The fourth element is maintaining a strong kicking game. We put our best players on these teams. The kicking game receives special emphasis.

In this chapter, we will focus on the red zone and, more specifically, the two-point conversion. A team may not need to attempt a two-point conversion for several games, but when they need a two-point conversion it is usually critical. We prepare four two-point plays during summer camp that we carry with us throughout the season. Practice and prepare for these situations so that your team knows the play before it is even called in the huddle.

In our system, the red zone is the 25-yard line on in. In this area on the field more than any other, variables change drastically. Often teams display distinct tendencies once they enter the red zone. For one thing, defensive behavior usually changes. Defensive coordinators often get more aggressive as the ball moves closer to their goal line. As you get deeper in the red zone, the vertical stretch that you can put on a defensive secondary changes drastically. Coverage zones get tighter as the field gets smaller. Coverage techniques change and usually the defensive backs and linebackers provide little or no cushion. The passing game becomes more condensed the closer you get, and the depth of routes and the quarterback's read need to be adjusted. Safety alignments become tighter, affecting the running game.

Each staff needs a red-zone philosophy that they discuss thoroughly before the game plan. We take an aggressive approach to the red zone: We have a clear goal of scoring touchdowns and not field goals. This goal is reflected in shots taken to the end zone and the four-down area in which we position ourselves on third down in order to make a fourth-down conversion.

The Call

For many years, the two-point conversion has been an integral part of high school and college football. In 1997, the NCAA added overtime to avoid ties. The rules state that if a game reaches a third overtime situation, both teams have to attempt two-point conversions after scoring because it is much more difficult to make a two-point conversion than an extra point. The NFL introduced the two-point conversion in 1999.

When and when not to attempt a two-point conversion has been the source of great debate among fans and coaches for many years. Staff members have a chart to help them make decisions in the heat of the moment. This chart lists several situations in which the decision to kick or go for two has been discussed in great detail (table 6.1). The chart isn't perfect, however. It doesn't account for the time, personnel, momentum, and location (home or visitors). For example, if the chart says to go for two but it is still early in the game, we often kick the extra point to ensure that we get points.

In the NFL, the national average for success on a two-point conversion is 43 percent versus 94 percent when kicking the extra point. In the NCAA, the two-point conversion is successful 43.5 percent of the time versus 93.8 percent when kicking the extra point.

Your coaching staff will face several critical decisions over the years. In the following sections, I detail two similar situations, break down the decision process, and then describe the outcome of each.

Table 6.1 **Two-Point Conversion or Extra Point Chart**

Points ahead	Extra point	Two-point conversion	Points behind	Extra point	Two-point conversion
0	X		−0	X	
1			−1	X	
2	X		−2		X
3	X		−3	X	
4		X	−4	X	
5*	(X)	(X)	−5		X
6	X		−6	X	
7	X		−7	X	
8	X		−8	X	
9	X		−9	X	
10	X		−10		X
11	X		−11	X	
12		X	−12		X
13	X		−13	X	
14	X		−14	X	
15	X		−15	X	
16	X		−16		X
17	X		−17	X	
18	X		−18		X
19		X	−19	X	
20	X		−20	X	
21	X		−21	X	
22		X	−22		X
23	X		−23		X
24	X		−24		X
25		X	−25		X
26	X		−26		X
27	X		−27		X
28	X		−28		X

*Consider according to the team's strengths.

Going for the Win

On November 17, 2001, Bowling Green was playing at Northwestern. Bowling Green was trailing Northwestern 42 to 28 with 3:40 left to play. After a Bowling Green score and extra point, the score was 42 to 35. Following a Northwestern turnover, Bowling Green went on to score a touchdown with 35 seconds left, putting the score at 42 to 41.

The staff made the decision to go for the two-point conversion even before the turnover. Here were the deciding factors:

1. Bowling Green was playing a Big Ten opponent on the road. Northwestern was a talented team, and the atmosphere was difficult. These two factors clearly made Bowling Green the underdog, so they wanted to end the game by going for the win rather than the tie.

2. Momentum had clearly shifted to Bowling Green in the fourth quarter.

3. The Northwestern defense was having difficulty containing the Bowling Green offense.

4. The Bowling Green defense had struggled the entire game against an explosive Northwestern offense.

Bowling Green's offensive players did not leave the field; they knew they would attempt the two-point conversion and they knew which play would be called after the touchdown. The two-point conversion (nine-zone Z-reverse pass, figure 6.1) was successful, and Bowling Green won the game 43 to 42.

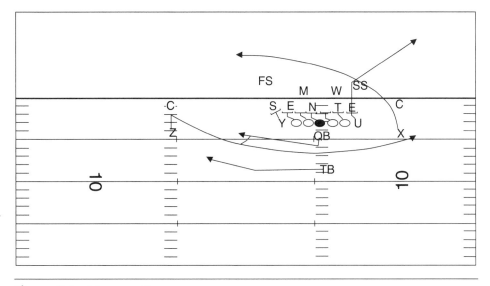

Figure 6.1 Nine-zone Z-reverse pass.

X: Nasty split; run 6-yard grag route.

Z: Nasty split; run reverse course; take the pitch from QB; run ball or throw to U in corner.

U: Slow release, block defensive end; run corner route to back corner of end zone.

Y: Block EMOL.

TB: Run 9-zone course.

QB: Run 9-zone course, dead pitch to Z.

PST: Block play-side gap; build wall; stay on line of scrimmage.

PSG: Block play-side gap; build wall; stay on line of scrimmage.

C: Block play-side gap; build wall; stay on line of scrimmage.

BSG: Block play-side gap; build wall; stay on line of scrimmage.

BST: Block play-side gap; build wall; stay on line of scrimmage.

The reverse play allowed Bowling Green to take advantage of the defense's aggressiveness on the goal line. Two tight ends protected Bowling Green off both sides. The ability to pass off the reverse allowed Bowling Green to make a good play if the defense stayed home on the backside.

Playing Overtime

On November 1, 2003, the University of Utah was playing Air Force at the Air Force Academy. Utah dominated the first half and went into halftime with a lead, 21 to 7. Air Force took control in the second half, tying the score at 28. Momentum had clearly shifted on both sides of the ball. Utah's offense and defense dominated Air Force the first 30 minutes with an overwhelming possession advantage of 21 minutes to 9 minutes. However, soon the Utah offense began to struggle to move the ball and the Utah defense began to show signs of fatigue as Air Force took control. Air Force had an opportunity to win the game late in the fourth quarter, but Utah blocked a 42-yard field goal attempt with 0:14 left to play.

The game went to overtime. Utah deferred and played defense first. Air Force scored quickly and elected to kick the extra point. Utah scored on the next possession and elected to kick the extra point for the following reasons:

1. In the second half, momentum had clearly shifted to Air Force.
2. The Utah offense had struggled significantly during the last five possessions against a very confident Air Force defense.

3. The Utah defense showed signs of having the ability to stop Air Force.

4. Utah had a size advantage on Air Force and felt they eventually could wear Air Force down if the game went to multiple overtimes.

The second overtime began with Utah scoring on the second play and once again electing to kick the extra point. Air Force went on to drive the ball to the 8-yard line and scored on a play-action pass. They elected to kick the extra point and force a third overtime.

According to NCAA rules, once the game entered the third overtime both teams had to attempt a two-point conversion after scoring. In the third overtime, Air Force drove the ball to the 2-yard line and scored on an option play to the left. Air Force failed on their attempt to make the two-point conversion, and Utah took over on the 25-yard line. A completed pass put the ball on the 3-yard line, first and goal. After three straight runs failed to score, Utah faced a fourth and goal situation from the 1-yard line. Utah took a time-out to discuss the play and decided to use a direct snap to the 255-pound halfback on an off-tackle power play they had used six or seven times earlier in the game. The play was successful and tied the score at 43. For the two-point conversion, Utah called for the same formation, using a direct snap to the halfback. This time, however, the halfback faked the run and threw a pop pass to the tight end (figure 6.2). The play was successful, and Utah won the game 45 to 43.

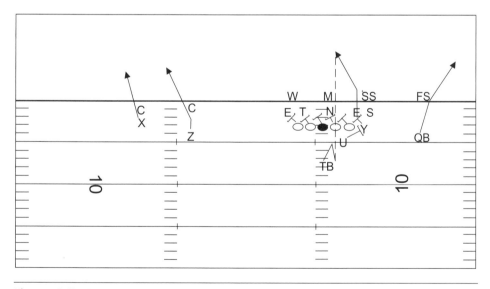

Figure 6.2 Pop pass.

X: Run a fade.

Z: Run a fade.

U: Block D-gap.

Y: Block backside gap and then release to up right.

TB: Fake 16 power pop-up and throw to Y.

QB: Walk up under the center then flex out strong and run a fade.

PST: Block backside gap; build wall; stay on line of scrimmage.

PSG: Block backside gap; build wall; stay on line of scrimmage.

C: Block backside gap; build wall; stay on line of scrimmage.

BSG: Block backside gap; build wall; stay on line of scrimmage.

BST: Block backside gap; build wall; stay on line of scrimmage.

This play begins by running a direct-snap power play to the tailback. The defense is forced to play aggressively on the run because the offense is in an empty formation. The defense also does not expect the tailback to throw a pass.

Two-Point Plays

The following two-point plays are plays we have used on several occasions. We always have three plays that we have practiced and tested during spring practice and training camp. Our team has confidence in these plays because they have practiced them in live situations and have seen them succeed. Our goal is for players to know what play will be called in different situations because they have rehearsed those situations many times. When developing our two-point package for the season, we consider several variables.

The first variable is personnel. We want a quarterback who can spread out the defense and still run base plays without extra defenders in the box. We want receivers who can create mismatches and expose the defender who has shown weakness in coverage. We want a physical offensive line because a lot of options are open to us if we can consistently run the ball for 3 yards. Finally, we want a great back.

The second variable is our opponent. We scout our opponents during the spring and summer and analyze their defense. What style of defense have they shown in two-point situations? Is there a weaker defender or area of the defense that we want to attack? Will the defense bring pressure or not?

The third variable is an all-purpose play that we can use from week to week so that the team has confidence in it. They will also know the play before it is called in the huddle since they have been preparing for it for several weeks.

The philosophy behind the 16-17 Q counterplay (figure 6.3) is to show a pass formation to the defense. The back's quick motion prevents the defense from having time to adjust. The gap scheme allows players to pick up different looks and pressures. The counteraction slows down defensive flow. If you have an athletic quarterback, this play puts the ball in his hands.

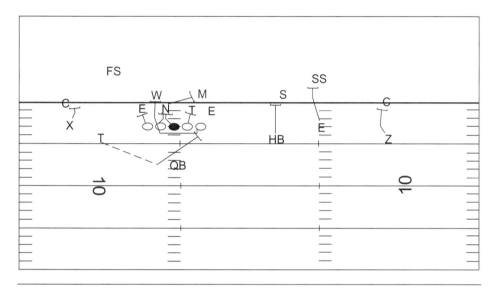

Figure 6.3   16-17 Q counterplay.

X: Stalk man over; free safety support; man on, inside numbers; backside cut off.

Z: Stalk man over; free safety support; man on, inside numbers; backside cut off.

HB: Stalk man over; free safety support; man on, inside numbers; backside cut off.

E: Stalk man over; man on, backside 4; free safety support; man on, inside numbers; backside cut off.

TB: Motion to backfield; cross in front of quarterback; flash fake; cut EMOL.

QB: Open to tackle; flash fake; get on puller's hip; run to daylight.

PST: Covered, man on.

PSG: Covered, man on; uncovered, scoop to backside linebacker.

C: Work tight shade to backside linebacker; versus odd scoop to backside linebacker.

BSG: Covered, man on; uncovered, inside slip to backside linebacker.

BST: Pull and lead up on front-side linebacker.

The philosophy behind the stick seam play (figure 6.4) is that the back's quick motion does not allow the defense time to adjust to the empty formation. This is an all-purpose route that can be used to attack both man and zone coverage. It is a great concept to use against goal-line coverage. The quarterback can take advantage of any mismatches with the defense.

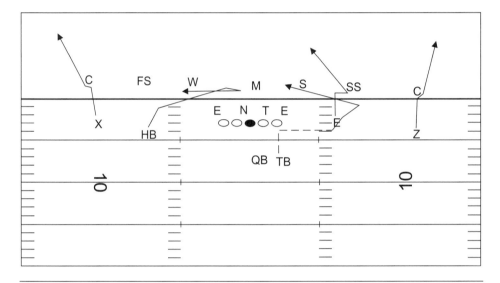

Figure 6.4 Stick seam.

X: Fade.

Z: Fade.

HB: Run a 5-yard pivot; try to draw out the backside linebacker; must win man-to-man.

E: Run a 5-yard stick seam.

TB: Motion to C-gap; run an angle route.

QB: Against zone, high or low read the front-side linebacker and check down to the pivot; against man, read the rub front-side and check down to the pivot; against game-plan matchup, throw fade to the outside.

PST: Block five-man protection.

PSG: Block five-man protection.

C: Block five-man protection.

BSG: Block five-man protection.

BST: Block five-man protection.

The sprint-right option play (figure 6.5) allows the quarterback to get outside and provides multiple options for attacking the defense. Using motion, the players create a rub when facing a man-to-man team and flood an area when facing a zone team. This is an all-purpose play that you can use from week to week no matter what type of defensive scheme you face.

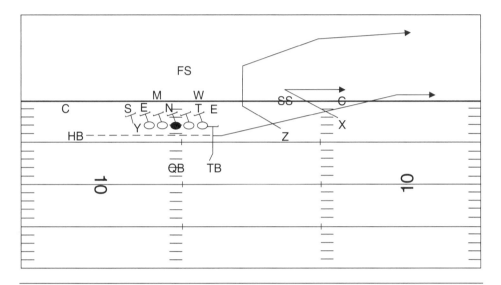

Figure 6.5   Sprint-right option.

X: Align 7 yards inside hash; create rub for H 2 yards into end-zone work area.

Z: Split the difference between Y and X; create rub; work into end zone; mirror quarterback.

HB: Align left motion to C-gap (snap point); run flat route; look for rub.

Y: Secure backside gap.

TB: Align toes 5 1/2 yards behind tackle; cut D-gap defender.

QB: Movement key is the flat defender; rub versus man; progression is H-X-Z to run; sprint, break contain.

PST: Secure backside gap.

PSG: Secure backside gap.

C: Secure backside gap.

BSG: Secure backside gap.

BST: Secure backside gap.

CHAPTER 7

© Virginia Tech

PUNT AND FIELD GOAL BLOCKS

BUD FOSTER
Virginia Tech

The quickest way to change the momentum of a football game is to create a big play in the kicking game. A blocked kick, long punt return, or kick-off return can change the momentum and demoralize your opponent. At Virginia Tech, the kicking game, specifically blocking kicks, has been as important to our success as any other part of the game. We have blocked 101 kicks—52 punts, 28 field goals, and 21 extra points—in 200 games. Almost all have led to a momentum swing and victory.

Rushing the Punt

Our punt return unit focuses on three types of plays: rushes, returns, and a combination rush and return. We have designed all three from one front to prevent our opponent from predicting what type of rush or return we are using. Players must understand that we want to sell the look that we are always bringing pressure. We want to put pressure on the punter, snapper, and entire punt unit at all times. This helps our rushes as well as sets up our returns.

Finally, we are offensive-minded in this phase of the game. This is an opportunity for us to score or gain valuable field position, and it is vital that we look at it in that respect. We want to set ourselves up to create big plays that help us win the game.

Personnel

The most important part of any phase of the game, including the kicking game, is selecting the right personnel for the unit. All of the players in the punt return unit must be potential kick blockers. The players we select for this unit must be dependable, fast, and good athletes in the open field.

We typically select athletes in skill positions, such as wide receivers, defensive backs, running backs, tight ends, and linebackers. We have used some of our defensive ends because of their ability to get off on the snap of the ball. These athletes usually have the speed and the athletic ability required to make this unit successful. However, over the years we have found that the best athletes may not be the best kick blockers. Certain players just have a special knack for blocking kicks. A good kick blocker needs timing, decision-making skills, and courage.

Drills

As with any other position, we use a series of drills to identify potential kick blockers and to teach players the necessary techniques.

The main drill we use to identify potential kick blockers is the block drill. We usually do this drill in spring practice and during the first couple of two-a-day practices in the fall. This drill requires four cones and three soft footballs. We deflate some old balls or use Nerf balls so as not to bang up the players' hands. Place four cones approximately 2 yards apart. At the start of the drill, a long snapper gets in position between the two middle cones. Divide the group of potential blockers and align them at the cones on both sides of the snapper (figure 7.1). We usually align faster players on the farthest cone and align players such as linebackers and defensive ends next to the center. Then we talk to the group about our basic rush principles.

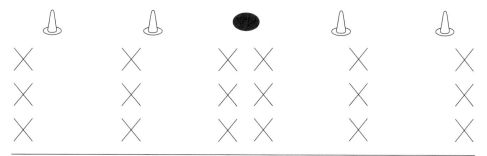

Figure 7.1 Block drill setup.

1. *Crowd the ball.* Players align as close as possible to the neutral zone without being offside. We tell players to keep their hands out in front of their heads, which should keep them from lining up offside.

2. *Key the ball.* Players must get a great jump on the ball. In order to do this, they must key the football in their peripheral vision and move when the snapper moves the ball.

3. *Stay low when charging, like a sprinter.* We also tell players to make themselves small. Players should run to the leg of the target, not the gap. The next drill works on this technique.

4. *Run through the block point.* We give players a new block point every week. The block point is based on whether the punter is a two-step or three-step kicker and how deep he goes from the line of scrimmage. The block point is generally 1 1/2 yards in front of the kicker's plant foot. We want players to rush through the block point, but never go deeper than the block point.

5. *Take the ball off the kicker's foot.* Players explode off the ball and accelerate through the block point. At the last second, they stick out their hands, put their hands together, and look to take the ball off the kicker's foot. We do not want players to turn their head or close their eyes. We also do not want them to slap at the ball. We want them to take the ball off the kicker's foot.

6. *Do not leave your feet*. We do not want players to leave their feet to block a kick. Once a player leaves his feet, he loses control of his body. If he is off course from the block point, he will rough the kicker.

In the block drill, one player goes at a time as determined by the coach. One coach stands on the line of scrimmage, checking stance, alignment, and getoff. Another coach stands behind the punter to evaluate the punt rusher, looking at his head and eyes and watching for correct execution of basic blocking techniques. The center snaps the ball or simulates the snap and the blocker executes his rush-and-block technique (figure 7.2).

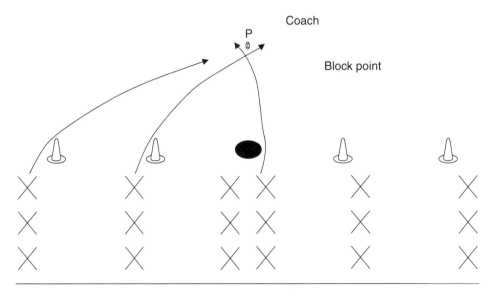

Figure 7.2   In the block drill, the center snaps the ball and the blocker rushes.

At this point we can determine who the punt blockers are and begin to teach them our basic rushes and returns. We look for quickness off the ball and we also consider the blocker's running pattern, the way he uses his eyes, and his hand placement.

The next drill we do is called run the leg. This drill teaches athletes to make themselves small as they rush their lanes, and it also teaches them to pick up their feet as they cross the line of scrimmage to block the kick.

Regardless of the type of protection (zone or man), players need to stretch the area to make it tougher to block the punt rusher. In this drill, we set up a punt protection unit and align them in a tight formation. We place half-round dummies between the blockers (figure 7.3). Then we talk to players about running the leg of the blocker, not the gap. Rushers must pick up their feet so they do not get tripped up by the blocker's legs.

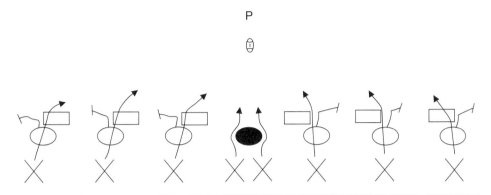

Figure 7.3 Run the leg drill.

You may wonder why we run the leg instead of the gap. If you run the gap, you put yourself closer to the blocking threat. By running the leg, you remove yourself from the blocking threat, forcing the blocker to stretch or move his inside foot to block you.

The drill begins with the center snapping the ball. We start one player at a time, progress to a half-line drill, and finish with the full group. The punt protection unit works to keep the inside foot planted and to step outside to protect their outside gap. On the snap, the rusher must get off on the ball and turn his body to make himself small so that he does not give the blocker a surface to get his hands on. The rusher must run over the inside leg of the man on him. At the same time he must pick up his feet by stepping over the leg and back of the man the rusher is aligned over. You can teach the drill in a progression by having the rusher run the leg only, then run the leg and block the kick. We teach players to run upfield close to the men over which they were aligned and then bend and run through the block point.

Rushes

Once we select personnel, we begin to teach rushes. We align players in specific areas by numbering personnel from left to right, 1 through 10 (figure 7.4). We also identify the punt unit according to position.

Our basic rush is a balanced 10-man rush (figure 7.5). We rarely send all 10, but all 10 must be potential kick blockers.

1, 10: Align approximately 1 yard outside the head hunter; attack the block point; block the kick.

2, 9: Align on the head hunter's outside shoulder; attack his outside number, run over his inside leg; block the kick.

3, 8: Align on the tackle's outside shoulder; attack his outside number, run over his inside leg; block the kick.

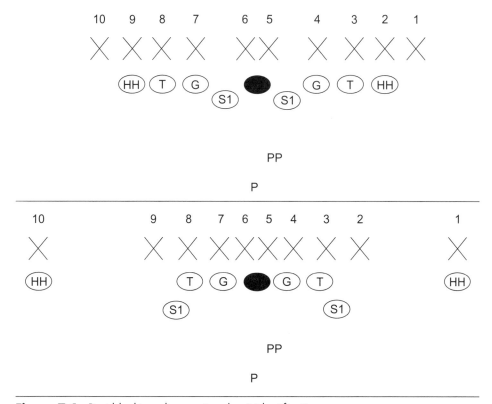

Figure 7.4 Punt blocking alignment and unit identification.

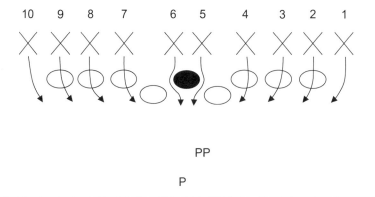

Figure 7.5 Balanced 10-man rush.

4, 7: Align on the guard's outside shoulder; attack his outside number, run over his inside leg; block the kick.

5, 6: Align tight to the center; swim the center, running as tight as possible to the center's near leg; block the kick.

Most teams use some kind of zone blocking scheme. The basic principle of running the leg is to create seams in zone protection by stretching blocking areas. In zone schemes, players are responsible for blocking the area to their outside. That is why we align so heavily on them. The player responsible for blocking a rusher is the player to his inside. That is why we run the leg and not the gap to stretch the area; it makes it tough for the blocker to block the rusher. We want to force the blocker to move his inside foot to block the rusher, which creates seams in the protection (figure 7.6).

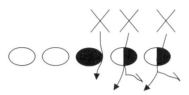

Figure 7.6 Create seams in the protection by forcing the blocker to move his inside foot.

Our numbering system allows us to determine who to send on rushes and who to check for potential fakes. When we call, "10-man rush, 1 and 10 stay," we send everyone except 1 and 10, who will check for a fake (figure 7.7).

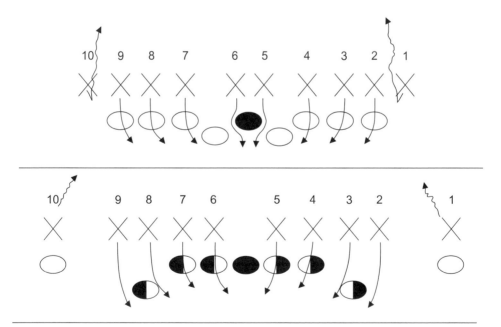

Figure 7.7 10-man rush, 1 and 10 stay to check for a fake.

The numbering system keeps things simple and allows us to use a variety of rush combinations, such as 1 and 10 stay, 4 and 7 stay (figure 7.8), 3 and 8 stay, and so on.

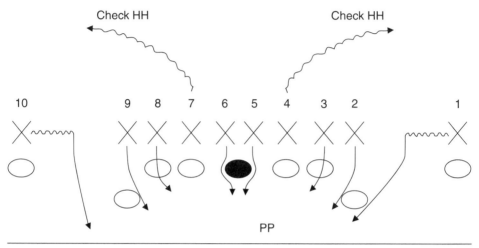

Figure 7.8 4 and 7 stay.

When we go for the block, we follow certain principles, depending on the situation:

1. On fourth down, if the ball is blocked and does not cross the line of scrimmage, players pick up the ball and run with it. If the team punts on third down, players fall on the ball unless it bounces up to a player in open space.

2. If the ball is blocked and crosses the line of scrimmage, players call "Peter" and get away from the ball.

3. If a player is picked up on his charge (blocked) or knocked off course by more than one step, he stops, staying square and moving to the outside. He does not continue on because he could get knocked into another rush lane and pick off a potential blocker. Ideally we want only one person free to the block point. We also do not want to knock the personal protector into the block point.

4. If the punt is not blocked, players use right returns unless we are using a combination rush and return. Players must sprint to set up the wall.

Combination Rush and Return

The ability to block kicks creates opportunities for the return game. You can use full returns or a combination rush and return. The rush and return (figures 7.9, 7.10, and 7.11) lets you pressure the punter and potentially block a kick, but it also forces the punt unit to stay in and block, allowing the return team to set up a good return.

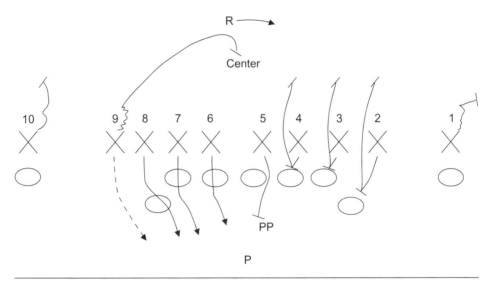

Figure 7.9 Rush right, return left.

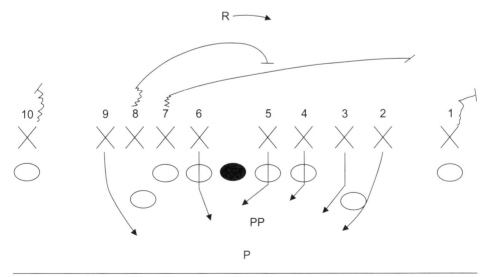

Figure 7.10 Rush left, return left.

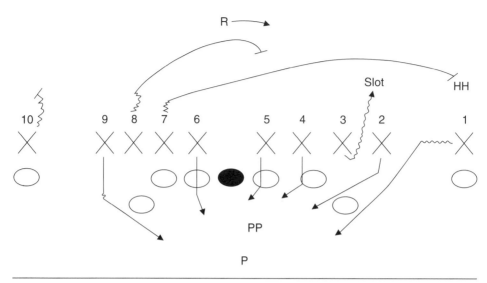

Figure 7.11 Rush left head hunter, return left.

1: Take the head hunter in the direction he wants to go and wall him away from the returner.

2, 3, 4: Block and trail, forcing your men away from the side of the return.

5: Swim the center and tie up the personal protector; block him away from the side of the return.

6, 7, 8: Run the inside leg of the men over you, blocking the kick; if the ball is kicked, work for width and get downfield approximately 5 yards apart; set up a wall to the side of the return.

9: Punch out at the snap, spying on the slot to your side for a fake; pick up the center and wall him away from the side of the return.

10: Force the head hunter to the outside and wall him away from the side of the return.

1: Take the head hunter in the direction he wants to go and wall him away from the returner.

2, 3, 4, 5, 6: Run the inside leg of the men over you, blocking the kick; if the ball is kicked, work for width and get downfield approximately 5 yards apart; set up a wall to the side of the return.

7: Punch out a second before the snap; check the slot to the side of the return for a fake; double-team the head hunter with 1.

8: Punch out a second before the snap; check the personal protector for a fake; be the spy for the returner; force would-be defenders away from the side of the return approximately 25 to 30 yards downfield.

9: Force the kick while checking the slot to your side for a fake; get into the wall.

10: Force the head hunter away from the side of the return.

The rush left head hunter, return left (figure 7.11) is similar to rush left, return left. The exception is that 1 is involved in the rush. We use the rush unit's prowling to create different alignments in order to confuse the protection unit. This also helps us align to attack any weaknesses we may have found during film study.

Blocking Extra Points and Field Goals

We use the same philosophy to attack placement kicks as we do punts. We work hard to block these kicks because points are involved. Blocking an extra point or causing a bad snap can lead your team to victory. We have blocked as many placement kicks as we have punts. This is a key play in the game, and our players take it seriously.

The biggest difference between blocking an extra point or field goal and blocking a punt is that players can leave their feet to block an extra point or field goal. We still give players a landmark. Because of the operation time of the field goal protection unit, we allow players to leave their feet.

One drill we use to work on blocking placement kicks is the mat drill (figure 7.12). We set up this drill primarily for the edge rushers. We set up a field goal unit (half line) and simulate a snap. We place a large mat opposite the rusher. The ball is snapped and players lay out, using their bodies as a surface area to block the kick. We do not want them to dive straight out; we want them to turn their bodies to create a broader surface to block the kick.

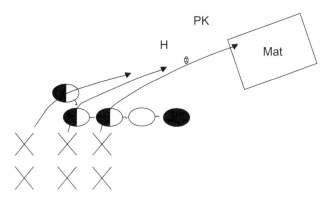

Figure 7.12 Mat drill.

We use edge rushes in addition to blocking up the middle. The fundamentals of stance alignment and getoff are the same as in punt blocks. Players must still run the leg of the man over them. Most extra point and field goal units step hard inside, so we run the outside leg or near leg we are aligned on. Figure 7.13 illustrates the block left or right play. We use the block left or right and the block left or right switch (see page 117) for changeups, especially if the tight end is outside-gap conscious (ricochet block).

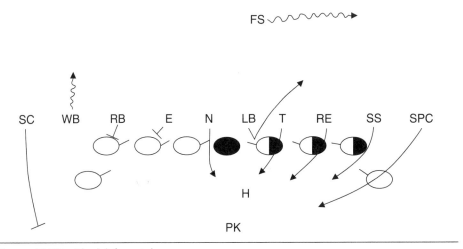

Figure 7.13 Block left or right.

SPC: Line up as end man on line of scrimmage to the side of the block; face in and drive through the wing's outside hip; lay out for the kick 1 yard in front of the ball placement.

SS: Align on the tight end's outside shoulder; run over his outside leg, expecting to block the kick.

RE: Align on the tackle's outside shoulder; run over his outside leg, expecting to block the kick.

T: Align on the guard's outside shoulder; run over his outside leg, expecting to block the kick.

LB: Shade the center to the side of the block; draw the guard's block; punch out; take on first inside receiving threat to the side of the block.

N: Shade the center opposite the block; attack the guard, staying square; be solid for a fake or penetrate to block the kick.

E: Align opposite the block; attack the tackle, staying square, looking for a fake.

RB: Align opposite the block; attack the tight end; cover the tight end man-to-man.

WB: Align opposite the rush; punch out; cover the wing man-to-man.

SC: Align opposite the rush; check alignment for offsides; sprint to a landmark 2 yards in front of ball placement; be under control, looking for a blocked kick or fake.

FS: Prowl; you have the first outside receiving threat to the side of the block.

You may use some of your inside personnel to punch out or loop around to protect against a fake.

If a team's tight end is more outside conscious in his protections, we run what we call the block left or right switch (figure 7.14). Everyone has the same responsibilities except the rush end and the strong safety. We blast out or pull the tight end with the rush end and run the strong safety over the outside leg of the tackle.

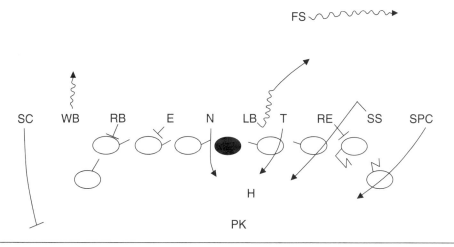

Figure 7.14 Block left switch.

We like using the block middle play (figure 7.15) for longer field goal attempts; generally the flight of the ball has a lower trajectory.

SPC: Align to the side of the block; punch out; cover the wing man-to-man.

SS: Align to the side of the block; cover the tight end man-to-man.

RE: Align to the side of the block; blast the tackle pad-under-pad.

T, N: Align to the side of the block; blast the guard pad-under-pad.

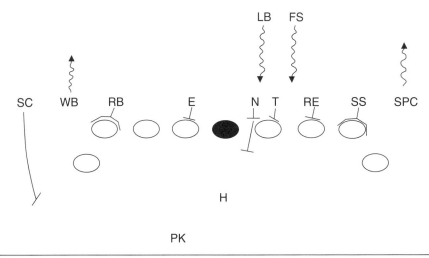

Figure 7.15 Block middle, left or right.

E: Align opposite the block; blast the guard pad-under-pad.

RB: Align opposite the block; cover the tight end man-to-man.

WB: Align opposite the block; punch out; cover the wing man-to-man.

SC: Align opposite the rush; check the alignment for offsides; sprint to a landmark 2 yards in front of the ball placement; be under control, looking for a blocked kick or fake.

FS, LB: Align 2 to 5 yards behind the defensive front to the side of the block; time snap by looking at the holder; attack the line of scrimmage, getting vertical; block the kick.

Creating a Weekly Practice Schedule

Football breaks down into three parts: offense, defense, and special teams. We want to make sure we get plenty of work with our special teams units. We also want players to know that special teams are as important to our success as offense and defense. We do this by working our special team units in the middle of practice rather than at the beginning or end. This places equal emphasis on all phases of the game.

We practice some aspect of special teams every day. Here is our daily practice schedule.

Monday (emphasis on special teams)

Period	Flex 10 minutes
1 (5 minutes)	Team converge
2 (5 minutes)	FG versus FG block (good versus good)

3 (10 minutes)	Individual
4 (10 minutes)	Pass skel
5 (10 minutes)	Punt protection (good versus good)
6 (10 minutes)	Punt rush (good versus good)
7 (25 minutes)	Team goal line, short yardage, blitz
8 (10 to 15 minutes)	Conditioning

Tuesday

Period	**Flex 10 minutes**
Specialty (10 minutes)	Punt, kickoff, returners, punt protection
1 Individual	Tackle, block protection
2 Individual	Fundamentals
3 Individual	Fundamentals
4 Individual	Fundamentals
5 Group work	One on one, skel, half line, and so on
6 Group work	One on one, skel, half line, and so on
7 Group work	One on one, skel, half line, and so on
8 Group work	One on one, skel, half line, and so on
9	Team versus scouts
10	Kicking, punt protection versus punt rush (good versus good)
11	Team versus varsity
12	Team versus scouts
13	Conditioning

Wednesday

Period	**Flex 10 minutes**
Specialty (10 minutes)	Punt, kickoff, returners, punt block
1 (10 minutes)	Individual
2 (10 minutes)	Individual
3 (10 minutes)	Individual
4 (10 minutes)	Inside versus scouts
5 (10 minutes)	Skel
6 (10 minutes)	Skel

7 Kick period

1. Punt protection versus punt rush (rush) (good versus good)
2. FG versus FG block (good versus good)
3. Punt protection versus punt rush (return) (good versus good)

4. Onside prevent versus air
5. Punt protection versus punt rush (rush) (good versus good)
6. FG versus FG block (good versus good)
7. Punt safe versus punt protection
8. Punt protection versus punt rush (return) (good versus good)
9. Kickoff return (squib or pooch kick)

8 (10 minutes)	Team versus scout
9 (10 minutes)	Team versus varsity, pass under pressure
10 (10 minutes)	Team versus scout
11 (10 minutes)	Team versus varsity, third and long
12 (10 minutes)	Team versus scout
Conditioning	Work some aspect of the kicking game such as punt return or kickoff coverage

Thursday (emphasis on kicking game)

Period	**Flex 10 minutes**
1 (10 minutes)	Kickoff return
2 (10 minutes)	Kickoff coverage
3 (5 minutes)	Punt rush, block kicks
4 (10 minutes)	Red-zone skel
5 (5 minutes)	Goal-line skel
6 (10 minutes)	Punt protection, fake or punt safe versus scout
7 (10 minutes)	Two-minute drill (good versus good)
8 (10 minutes)	Team
9 (10 minutes)	Team
10 (10 minutes)	Team

Friday

Flex (10 minutes)

Individual (10 minutes)

Central meeting (5 minutes)

Punt protection

1. Poocher
2. Kick out of the end zone
3. Kick at 5 seconds, take time off the clock
4. 11-man rush, rocker kick
5. Take a safety

Kickoff return
1. Pop up or pooch kick
2. Squib
3. After a safety (punter)

Punt rush
1. Get a jump
2. Kick blocked, behind or past line of scrimmage
3. Return versus short kick, "Peter" call
4. Fake

FG block
1. Get a jump
2. Kick blocked, behind or past the line of scrimmage

FG protection
1. Jump on snap, steps
2. Cover

Kickoff coverage
1. Get a jump, cover
2. Onside
3. After a safety (punter)

Punt safe
1. Get a jump
2. Return

As you can see, we work good versus good as much as possible throughout the week. We do not have a lot of players crossing over, especially when the punt protection unit goes against the punt rush unit or the field goal protection goes against the field goal block. This creates a gamelike tempo. If we use our personnel in both units, we emphasize one unit over the other and work against backups or a scout unit.

Special teams can play a major role in determining the outcome of a ball game. The team that wins two of the three aspects of the game usually wins the game. The next time you hear the crowd yelling, "Block that kick," think of the effect that play will have on the outcome of the game.

CHAPTER 8

© Human Kinetics

DEVELOPING SPECIAL TEAMS UNITS

MIKE SABOCK
Northern Illinois University

A team doesn't automatically have a great kicking game just because it has a good kicker or punter, just as its offense does not flourish just because it has a good quarterback. A quarterback must have great pass protection, a complimentary running game, blitz checks, and more. The kicking game also must meet certain criteria if it is to give a team a winning edge.

Successful special teams have four elements: mistake elimination, positive attitude and effort, solid fundamentals, and sufficient practice time.

As in every aspect of football, elimination of mistakes is a key to sustained success. With special teams, avoiding mistakes is even more important. A player on the punt team may only get five opportunities in a game to do his job. If he is perfect four out of five times, he is successful 80 percent of the time. In school, 80 percent is a B- or C, an average performance that does not lend itself to a winning effort.

Most mistakes in the kicking game are the result of underestimating the kicking game's importance. Either the coaches accept small mistakes, or the players relax a little and get sloppy. Coaches must demand perfection in the kicking game. Players need to understand that they must perform on game day or the team could lose the game.

Special teams players who have great talent but put forth average effort could cost you the game. We have all seen some of the best athletes take a breather when it is their time to perform in the kicking game. A coach's job is to instill the intensity required to get the job done. Many backup players are great special teams players because they are fresh and go 100 percent. If a coach can get his most talented players to play on special teams at 100 percent, it increases their chance for success. The attitude and effort that the players bring to the game are the direct result of what the coaches demand. When a team covers punts in practice, do the coaches stand and watch or do they chase them down the field? At Northern Illinois we talk about the wow factor. When our kickoff team sprints down the field and makes the play, we coaches want to stand on the sideline and say "Wow!"

Kickers and punters need to have perfect fundamentals in order to achieve perfection. Most coaches understand that fact even if they don't understand what those fundamentals are. The fundamentals that must be coached well are protecting kicks, blocking during returns, holding up players on returns, blocking kicks, and so on. Players not only need to know what to do but how to do it. Teaching these kicking game fundamentals is no different than teaching fundamentals to offensive and defensive linemen or the quarterback and defensive back.

A successful kicking game requires practice. Unfortunately, many coaches have difficulty giving special teams enough practice time. In a normal practice session, head coaches allow time for individual techniques, group work, and team work. Many of these same coaches only assign team time to the kicking game. It is just as important for special teams players to practice individual techniques as it is for offensive linemen to practice individual techniques before moving into the team phase of practice. Special team practice must be extremely organized so as to not waste any valuable time.

Special Teams Coaching

There are three ways to run a special teams unit. The first is to have a special teams coordinator who is in charge of every phase of the kicking game. He decides which schemes and fundamentals to teach and who is responsible for implementing them.

The second way is to have a special teams coordinator who oversees all the units but assigns other coaches to be the head coach of individual units. Each unit's head coach reports to the special teams coordinator.

The third way is to have no special teams coordinator. The head coach assigns the units to coaches, putting them in charge of their phase of the kicking game. This is an important decision to make. Every staff has coaches who have some expertise in special teams and enjoy that part of the game. Every staff also has coaches who don't have any expertise in the kicking game and don't care. You need someone running the show who is a kicking game expert or is willing to do whatever it takes to gain that expertise.

Special Teams Coordinator

There are many benefits to having a special teams coordinator. If a head coach is lucky enough to have a coach on his staff who knows and loves the kicking game, having a special teams coordinator in charge of the entire kicking game is a good option.

The special teams coordinator is in charge of personnel, scheme, implementation, practice organization, and scouting reports. Anything to do with the kicking team is the responsibility of this coach. It is up to him to pick coaches to assist him with the different phases as he sees fit. This frees the other coaches to get the offensive and defensive work done.

It also frees the coaches during a game from gameday kicking adjustments. Any changes made during a game are handled by the special teams coordinator. When a player gets injured, the trainers go to the special teams coordinator and he makes the adjustment with the players. The special teams coordinator must be highly organized, highly motivated, and an expert in all the intricacies of the kicking game.

I once knew a head coach who appointed his tight ends coach as his special teams coordinator. He reasoned that the tight ends coach was the coach with the most free time. However, the tight ends coach had no expertise in the kicking game and minimal organizational skills. After one season of many kicking game miscues, the head coach made a change and hired the best man for the job rather than the one with the most extra time.

Special Teams Coordinator and Assistants

If the head coach has a few coaches on staff who have expertise in the kicking game, he may elect to assign them to different units. It is still possible to have a special teams coordinator who oversees all special teams units. The coordinator is in charge of the overall kicking game and the unit coaches report to him.

In this scenario, each coach acts as the head coach of his unit. One coach is in charge of the kickoff team, another is in charge of the punting team, and so on. Each individual coach is responsible for his unit's scheme, implementation, game plan, film analysis, and personnel.

The special teams coordinator oversees the whole process. He sets up the long- and short-term practice plans. He offers his expertise to the individual unit coaches, much like the team's head coach. The special teams coordinator is the head coach of the kicking game, and he counts on his assistants to get the job done in their units. Usually the special teams coordinator will coach two or three phases and assign the rest of the phases to other coaches. On game day, coaches run all decisions and adjustments by the special teams coordinator to keep communication smooth on the sideline.

Individual Coaches, Head Coach As Coordinator

Some head coaches do not feel that a special teams coordinator is necessary. When this is the case, the head coach must act as the coordinator. The head coach sets up all the practice schedules. He is responsible for personnel on game day. Individual coaches are in charge of their kicking units, but the head coach needs to pull it all together.

Some head coaches believe that this is a good way to handle special teams. They feel that it gets more coaches involved in the game plan and running the team. In team meetings, not just one coach talks, but each individual coach talks about his phase. Some head coaches believe that players respond better to different coaches rather than one coach.

One of the negatives of having no coordinator is that everything is its own entity. For personnel decisions, one person needs to look at the big picture to make sure players aren't stretched too thin. Each coach is going to want the best players in his unit. If every unit has the best players, players will be overworked and tired by the middle of the game. Someone must be in charge for the good of the whole team, so the head coach must act as the coordinator to make sure all phases are pulled together.

Another negative of having no coordinator is the confusion that results when an injury occurs during a game. Instead of coaching the game, four or five coaches may be on the headsets talking about who needs to go in for who on which kicking team. A coach on the sidelines has to run around and make adjustments on teams he might not even be involved with. With a special teams coordinator, this is never a problem because one coach handles all the adjustments. Everyone else can continue to do his job without worrying about adjustments.

Special Teams Personnel

Choosing the best players for the different phases of the kicking game is of the utmost importance. Sometimes the best athlete on the team is the best choice. At other times a third-team player with great desire is the best choice.

The first thing a coach must figure out is which starters have the conditioning and desire to play their positions and also excel in the kicking game. Some starters are short-winded and need to take a break during kicking situations. Other starters act like they never want to come off the field. The more starters you have who want to excel in the kicking game, the better. However, many backup players may do just as well or better in the kicking game because that is their thing to do. I have seen many players who run 40 yards in 4.8 seconds run down on a kickoff team and beat players who run 4.5. Why is this? Desire and conditioning.

It is imperative that you evaluate kicking team personnel each day. After practice, the first film I watch is the kicking film. I examine personnel and technique as I watch. Constantly check to make sure you are putting players on the field who give you the best effort and fundamentals. Do not be afraid to put a third-string player on the kicking team if he has a better chance of getting the job done.

One way to pick personnel is to use the scout teams. I always handpick the scout kicking teams. A lot of players come up to special teams coaches and say they want to be on a kicking team. When that happens to me, I put them on the scout kicking team and tell them to show me that they deserve a chance. I explain that we have limited repetitions in practice and until they prove to me that they deserve a shot, I can't afford to give them reps. A player who can help you win games on special teams ought to be tough to stop when he is on the scout team. When you practice punt protection, is there an athlete on the scout punt block team who always gets through? If so, you had better put him on your punt rush team! Is there a player who always messes up your kickoff return in practice by making every tackle? He is kickoff team material!

At some point before the games start, you need to practice each phase live. How else can you know if the chosen players will perform well in the heat of battle? The kicking game is no different than offense or defense. You must do it live before the first game. I would much rather find out in practice if I have to correct players than look at film after the first game and decide.

Practice Time

Whether coaches want to admit it or not, special teams tend to get the short end of the stick when it comes to practice time. If the kicking game is truly a third of the game, it should receive a third of the practice time. In a two-hour practice, one-third is 40 minutes. However, most teams do not spend 40 minutes on the kicking game during practice. Because of the limited amount of time, the time you do spend on the kicking game must be organized so not one single minute is wasted. Players need to know where they are going, coaches need to know what they are doing, and the kicking scout teams need to know who they are and be ready to go. Coaches should meet during the day to go over the plan. The special teams coordinator, head coach, individual unit coach, or whoever is in charge must let everyone know what they are going to do.

The coach in charge of the scout team must talk to each player and let him know where he needs to be and when. Managers should know the field setup (cones) and when it needs to be ready. There is nothing worse than spending the first 3 minutes of a 10-minute segment finding scout players who aren't there or setting up the drill. Time is too valuable to waste on organizational problems.

Most practices start with a specialist period. This is where punters punt, kickers kick, snappers snap, holders hold, and punt and kick returners catch. This is truly a phase for individual, specific skills within the kicking game. However, you can do so much more during a specialist period. You can set up a punt block drill. You can set up a drill for setting the wedge on kickoff returns. You can address punt team footwork. This is a great time to get individual work on a lot of areas of the kicking game. To do this, you must be extremely organized—you must know where people are on the field, what equipment is needed, what coaches are involved, and so on.

One problem with specialty periods is that players need to leave individual meetings early to get out to the field. A lot of position coaches resent this because they don't understand the importance of individual technique in the kicking game. It is up to the head coach to set the policy for everyone to follow. One solution to this problem is to have every player on the field at the same time during specialty periods. If individual players are not involved that day, they can have a walk-through meeting on the field with their coach. You should always be organized enough to cover individual technique. The coordinator should set up a schedule in advance of what techniques players will work on that day.

Once practice starts, decide when to fit the different kicking phases into the schedule. One philosophy is to start practice with kicking. This emphasizes the importance of the kicking game. It also allows the scout team to be ready at the start of practice so no time is spent rounding up players. Scout team players can have their scrimmage jerseys on ahead of time. The kickers are warmed up because they just finished their specialty period. Organizationally it is sound because the team is usually together during stretching.

Another philosophy is to mix kicking phases throughout practice. There are some good reasons behind this philosophy. Players need to be on their toes and ready when called on, making practice more gamelike. It is also a good way to break up the monotony of practice because you can move from an offensive or defensive phase to a kicking phase, back to a two-minute phase, then back to another kicking phase, and so forth. The disadvantage is that the scout team is not quite as ready because they are coming to the drill from different areas of the field wearing different jerseys. If a player has been injured during practice, the scout team coach may have to scramble to find a replacement. These are a few examples of how the organization can get thrown off when you intersperse special teams segments throughout the practice.

The last philosophy is to work the kicking phase at the end of practice. There are some advantages to this system. There is no more practice afterward, so all focus is on the kicking phase. You can take an extra minute or so to set up because it is the last thing you are doing. If you run over a few minutes, it doesn't throw off the whole practice schedule. Players not involved in the kicking game can work on conditioning, which is good because often players in the kicking game think they have to run more than their teammates. On the other hand, some coaches feel that practicing the kicking game last sends a message to the team that kicking is less important than offense and defense.

Whichever practice philosophy the head coach holds, he still has to sell the philosophy to the players. No matter where you place kicking in practice, the coach's enthusiasm will carry over to the players.

How to achieve practice repetitions is always a concern. How much time do starters get and how much time do backups get? You must determine this by practice time and who is in charge.

The one phase of the kicking game where starters and backups should always practice an equal number of repetitions is the punting team. If the starting punting team is going to see five punt rush looks in the next game, the backup punting team must also see these same five looks. All it takes is one injury and one unprepared substitute player to get a punt blocked. The punting team is made up of assignments and techniques. One small breakdown can be devastating. It doesn't matter if a player is a backup or not, he must be able to get the job done. In other phases of the kicking game, a backup who misses an assignment would probably not have such dire consequences.

As a coach, you need to decide how important it is to work the backups. Obviously the starters are going to be on the field most of the time so they need to be perfect. The backups need to be as sound in their assignments as you have time for.

A kicking game checklist (figure 8.1) is a valuable tool for a special teams coach. The list should include every aspect of each kicking team that must be practiced. It also needs to include all the unique things that can happen in a game.

Kickoff		**Kickoff Return**	
Deep right	___	Middle wedge	___
Deep left	___	Sideline right	___
Deep middle	___	Sideline left	___
Power kick	___	Surprise onside	___
Kangaroo kick	___	Squib kick	___
Surprise onside	___	After safety	___
Obvious onside	___	Pooch kick	___
Kickoff after safety	___		
Holding ball	___		
50-yard line	___		
Last play of the game	___		

Punt		**Punt Return**	
Spread punt	___	Safe	___
Tight punt	___	Middle block	___
Sky punt	___	Block right	___
Yellow call	___	Block left	___
Hold call	___	Sell out	___
Taking a safety	___	Wall right	___
		Wall left	___
		Middle return	___
		Peter call	___
		10-yard line	___

Figure 8.1 Kicking game checklist.

As with offense and defense, quality meeting time is essential. However, this part of the kicking game is often overlooked. Many coaches seem to think that all the teaching can be done on the field. This simply is not the case. The work accomplished in a meeting room eliminates unnecessary talking during practice, allowing more productivity on the field.

Players also must see themselves on videotape so they can make necessary improvements. We have all seen players who are shocked when they see themselves on film and realize they are performing a technique incorrectly, just as you have been telling them. They can see the mistake on the video, but they can't feel the mistake on the field. Even a 5- or 10-minute kicking meeting to show practice film will pay great dividends the next day in practice.

Game Preparation

When preparing a game plan, start by analyzing the upcoming opponent. At the beginning of the week, watch all of your opponent's kicking plays that you have on film. The first time through, get a feel for their philosophy.

Opponent's punting team

1. What is their base formation?
2. Do they use more than one formation?
3. Do they motion?
4. How is their getoff time?
5. Do they cover well?
6. Do they run fakes?

Opponent's punt return

1. How often do they try to block punts?
2. Are they good at blocking punts?
3. Are they more of a return team?
4. How good is their returner?
5. Do they use a sideline or middle return?
6. Do they use different looks in different games?
7. Are they predictable?

Opponent's kickoff

1. Where do they try to kick the ball?
2. How strong is the kicker's leg?
3. Will they surprise onside or pooch kick?
4. How disciplined is their coverage?

Opponent's kickoff return

1. How good is their returner?
2. What returns do they use?
3. Do the returns change from game to game?
4. Are they predictable?

Opponent's field goal

1. How good is their kicker?
2. Do they huddle?
3. Do they use a huddle that could turn into a formation for a fake?
4. Does the kicker get good height on the ball?

Opponent's field goal block

1. Are they a middle or edge block team?
2. Are they predictable?

These are some general concepts to think about the first time you look through the kicking film. As you watch and take notes you will begin to get a feel for their philosophy. Some teams change little from week to week but emphasize soundness. Other teams change weekly and sacrifice soundness for the element of surprise. Once you start to understand your opponent, you can begin to formulate your game plan.

The next time through the film, look at individuals. Look for the key players, and look for weaknesses you can exploit. After going through the films twice, you should have a handle on what you need to do and how you plan to get it done.

The pregame warm-up is the time to analyze your kicker and punter as well as your opponent's kicker and punter. Your kicker should kick at both ends of the field to get a feel for the wind conditions. Before the game starts, the coach in charge of the field goal team should determine the exact yard line the ball needs to be on in order to attempt a field goal from either end of the field. That yard line can vary 10 to 15 yards on a windy day. I have had tremendous success with kickers and a big part of my success is that I can get a strong sense of a kicker's capabilities from the pregame warm-up. It does not matter what the kicker has done in the past; it only matters what he can do in the current conditions.

I like to use a stopwatch with my punter during pregame punts. I time every punt he kicks with a snapper. We get punts off in 2.0 seconds from the snap to the kick. Some punters take their time during warm-ups, but I believe that is a bad habit. I stand right beside him and tell him his getoff time after every punt. This reinforces the idea that the punts in the game are no different than every other punt he kicks.

Someone should always be charting the opponent's punter and kicker. You want to get a feel for the kicker's distance in both directions. Into the wind, he may line drive the kick more, hinting that you should use the middle block. With the wind, he may be able to attempt a long kick, helping you be prepared for your substitution pattern during the game. Watch the snapper for any presnap movement you may have missed on film. Listen to the holder's cadence. You may pick up a tip that will help your rushers.

You want to get a feel for the opposing punter's distance in both directions. On film, you should have charted his kicks. Now you can judge him based on the wind conditions in a live situation. This is imperative for aligning the punt returner deep enough but not too deep.

By the time the game starts, your punter is ready, your field goal coach and offensive coordinator know what yard line to get to for a field goal attempt, your field goal block coach has a plan, and your punt returner knows exactly how deep to line up.

Regardless of how you designate coaching responsibility, someone must be in charge of each unit on the sideline. By far, the best method I have found for getting kicking teams huddled up, accounted for, and onto the field is a launch pad. I use a red carpet that is 4 yards by 3 yards. We position the launch pad at the 50-yard line. Every kicking unit except the field goal team huddles on the launch pad. The kickoff team and kickoff return team easily assemble on the launch pad because there usually is plenty of time. It is much more critical to get the punting team, punt return team, and field goal block team huddled up so that when a play ends you are ready to send the proper unit onto the field. Whoever is in charge cannot be a game spectator on third down. He must be on the launch pad, taking attendance while the third-down play is taking place. As the play ends, he must have the kicking unit ready to go.

The launch pad is a great reference point for any players involved in the kicking game. They know exactly where to be on third down if they are not in the game. After years of handling special teams, I have learned that this one small thing can eliminate needless game penalties and substitution errors.

Grading System

Many teams use helmet stickers to award players who perform well. These awards can be a great motivational tool for special teams players and can have even more meaning if the team earns awards only for special teams play.

To give out awards, you need a grading system. You can award points for a lot of different successes within a kicking phase. Table 8.1 is a sample system for awarding points. As you can see, the player with the ball can earn points, but more importantly, the surrounding cast can also earn points.

Table 8.1 **Special Teams Award System**

Play	Points earned	Play	Points earned
Kickoff team		**Kickoff return team**	
Outstanding team or individual play	10	Outstanding team or individual play	10
Kickoff into end zone and downed	5	Score	10
Forced fumble	5	30-yard return	5
Recovered fumble	5	Key block	4
Kickoff into end zone	3	Great effort	3
Kickoff inside 5-yard line	1	Grade 100 percent	3
Tackle inside 20-yard line	3	Missed assignment	−3
Great effort	3		
Tackle	2		
Grade 100 percent	3		
First man down	2		
Last man down	−2		
Loaf	−5		
Missed assignment	−3		
Punting team		**Punt return team**	
Outstanding team or individual play	10	Outstanding team or individual play	10
35-yard punt with no return	3	Score	10
Forced fumble	5	Block punt	10
Recovered fumble	5	20-yard return	5
Punt inside the 20	3	10-yard return	3
Great effort	3	Key block	4
Perfect snap	2	Great effort	3

Play	Points earned	Play	Points earned
Punting team		**Punt return team**	
Tackle	2	Grade 100 percent	3
Grade 100 percent	3		
Loaf	−5		
Missed assignment	−3		
FG–PAT		**FG–PAT**	
Outstanding team or individual play	10	Outstanding team or individual play	10
Score 6 points	10	Block kick	10
Great effort	3	Score	3
Perfect snap	1	Loaf	−5
Perfect hold	1		

10 points equals 1 helmet award.

There are a tremendous number of right ways to coach football. No one knows the only way! The key to successful special teams play is to use your staff's expertise, allocate the necessary practice time to fundamentals, and put players on the field who can execute the scheme with great effort and skill.

PART II

TECHNIQUES

DON NEHLEN

Experience has shown that teams who play well in the kicking game have a significant edge over their opponents. In addition, big plays in the kicking game excite the fans and make the stadium rock. Players feed off fan enthusiasm, playing with increased inspiration.

Part II of this book deals with kicking game fundamentals. In chapter 9, Jeff Hayes presents the art of punting the football. Coach Hayes breaks down the fundamentals in a way that is of tremendous value to any punters coach.

Coach Brian Polian from the University of Buffalo walks you through the fundamentals of extra point and field goal kicking. The information Coach Polian provides will greatly benefit the kickers coach.

Coach Bill Legg from Purdue University covers the fundamentals of snapping the football for the punt, field goal, and extra point. This chapter is a must-read for all line coaches who work with snappers.

Coach Steve Kidd from Rice University covers the fundamentals of holding for kickers, including areas that a lot of coaches overlook. One muffed snap can cost you the game.

All coaches will want to spend time on chapter 14. Coach Bill Lynch from DePauw University covers the fundamentals of catching punts and kickoffs.

In chapter 15, Joe DeForest from Oklahoma State University gives valuable insight into special team player development. Coach DeForest talks about the attitudes the players must possess to be on special teams. His philosophy on the kicking game is invaluable.

Enjoy part II of this book. Remember, special teams can win the game. The key is the commitment you demand from your staff and players.

CHAPTER 9

© Human Kinetics

PUNTING

JEFF HAYS

Catch a poor snap, kick a falling ball seconds before some of the best opposing players get it, kick the ball far and high in a variety of ways depending on field position, weather conditions, and opponent capabilities—it's a tough assignment, but a great punter who gets the job done can be the most valuable defensive player on the team. A punter who has mastered his craft can help you gain massive field position, negate a dangerous returner, limit opposing offenses, and get your team out of a hole. Like other positions, punters must possess talent, skill, and mental mastery to be successful, so that's how I've organized this chapter. Also like other positions, punters need coaching, so in addition to discussing the coaching points and drills relevant to each skill, I also discuss tools that will help you help your players help their team.

Talent

The best punters are built from a foundation of great athletic ability. The demands of the position require the punter to be one of the best overall athletes on the team. A punter must have good hands in order to catch all manner of snaps under all types of conditions—the consequences of failure can be disastrous. He must be flexible so that his leg strikes the ball with the highest possible speed and control. He must have quickness and explosiveness in order to grab a bad snap, get the ball off on time, and hit the ball high and far.

Although great punters come in many shapes and sizes, a taller punter gives the snapper a better margin for error, and the punter's longer limbs move his foot faster for a given muscular effort. The punter must be coordinated and able to repeat his performance so that the ball and his foot meet in about the same way every time. Finally, he must have discipline, mental toughness, and competitiveness. He must be good enough to compete at several positions, and he can certainly do more than punt. In short, if you want great results from your punter, start with a player who has a great athletic foundation.

Punting Skills

Punting is easy to understand but difficult to do. Keep it sufficiently simple (KISS) so that the punter can coach himself in the off-season and feel confident in his fundamentals when he's out there performing.

In accordance with the KISS philosophy, we can divide the mechanics into eight distinct elements: alignment and stance, catch, presentation, approach, drop, leg swing, plant-leg drive, and body position.

Alignment and Stance

Initial alignment depth depends on the snapper's ability and the team's scheme. Most punters align 13 to 15 yards deep, directly behind the center, shoulders perpendicular to the punt line or direction in which they are punting. For coffin corner or out of bounds punts, the punter may shift a yard away from the direction he's punting; for example, he may align slightly left when punting right (figure 9.1).

Figure 9.1   Alignment when punting to the right.

When punting at an extreme angle, the punter who fails to shift is in danger of having the punt blocked by the outside rush. However, aligning too far to the side will make it difficult for the snapper to execute the snap.

Punters begin in a modified athletic position with the feet comfortably shoulder-width apart, knees and hips slightly flexed, and weight slightly forward with shoulders over knees, knees over toes. The punter's feet may be parallel or slightly staggered depending on whether the punter uses a two-step approach (punting foot slightly forward) or a three-step approach (punting foot slightly back) (figure 9.2).

Figure 9.2 Three-step stance.

Initial hand and arm positions are irrelevant. However, the punter needs to be able to use his hands to communicate to the snapper that he is ready (hand flash) or not (we use the forearms crossed low in an X). The punter should stay relaxed and ready.

Catch

The punter needs to have hands like a wide receiver's: soft, secure, and reliable. The hand positions for catching high, low, and to the side snaps are similar to the hand positions used by a wide receiver. For example, the punter keeps his thumbs in if the snap is above the waist and pulls his thumbs apart if the snap is below the waist. Like a wide receiver, the punter also needs soft, relaxed hands and arms that give slightly with the snap. The differences are that the punter keeps the ball in front of him after catching it instead of tucking it away (figure 9.3), and the punter must be ready to bend at the knees and hips to field a low snap without touching his knee to the ground.

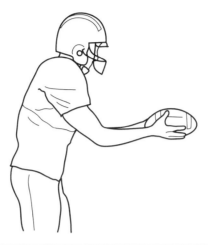

Figure 9.3 Athletic position, catching and keeping the ball in front.

The punter must perform like a baseball shortstop, vacuuming up everything that comes his way. If the snap is low, the punter must stop the ball and keep it in front of him. If the snap is over his head, the punter must do his best to chase the ball and get off the punt.

Standard wide receiver drills can improve a punter's catching skills. An around the world drill (figure 9.4), in which the punter passes the

Figure 9.4 Around the world drill.

ball around each leg and his waist 10 times both clockwise and counter-clockwise, helps the punter develop finger strength and a feel for the ball. Right and left quick turns, in which the punter stands 15 yards away with his back to the passer and the passer tells the punter to turn as he throws the ball, help tune visual focus and reaction to the snap. Playing catch while working on hand and body adjustment to high, low, left, and right balls allows the punter to handle the various types of snaps he might encounter. Finally, catching with a pole in front of him (figure 9.5) will help the punter hone his concentration and keep the ball away from his body. Practicing with the snapper, including bad snaps, also helps develop catching skills.

Figure 9.5 Pole in front drill.

The Jugs machine is an excellent tool for these drills; we use it daily. Punters also can work on catching and hand control through juggling, basketball, and similar activities.

Presentation

After catching the ball and holding it in front and away from his body, the punter molds the ball by rotating it so that the laces are where he wants them (usually directly on top so he can use them as a visual cue) and extending his arm so that the ball is away from him and over the hip of his punting foot (figure 9.6).

The grip—one hand or two and top, bottom, or side (figure 9.7)—is a matter of preference, although I prefer a single-handed side grip because it gives greater control and more visual landmarks (where the fingers

Figure 9.6 Proper presentation.

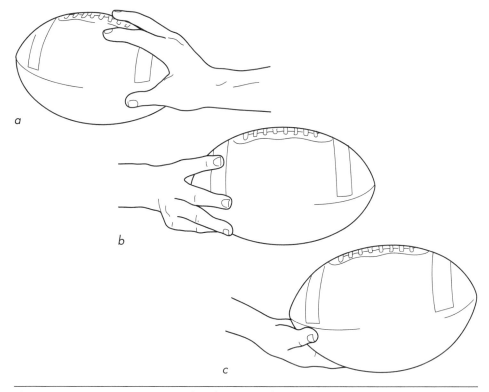

Figure 9.7 Grips: *(a)* top grip; *(b)* side grip; *(c)* bottom grip.

touch the ball). With a side grip, the punter should shake hands with the ball, gripping it with his fingertips, the nose of the ball barely touching his palm. The punter holds the ball in front of himself, elbow extended but not locked, wrist straight. Punters and coaches should use seams and stripes as visual landmarks to check the consistency of the grip (for example, middle finger on the seam, thumb on the stripe).

For a punt with equal height and distance, the seam of the ball should be parallel to the ground and at chest-height in the initial position of the basic drop. Imagine a plane passing through both side seams, parallel to the ground. This "drop plane" is an important concept for getting equal height and distance. Punters who want to drive the ball against the wind or farther with shorter hang time use a slightly depressed (nose toward the ground) drop plane. Punters who want to hang the ball higher use a slightly elevated drop plane (nose toward the sky).

Modifications of the drop plane begin with the presentation. The punter makes the ball fit the image he expects to see. He makes changes by shoulder movement only. The nose is turned in to get the butt of the ball away from the punter's shin and to give the foot a greater chance to hit the sweet spot. The amount the nose turns in depends on the position of the punter's foot at contact, which can be determined by viewing video shot from the front. A duck-footed punter can point the nose straighter than one who is more pigeon-toed, but both can be successful punters. A certain amount of trial and error is necessary to find the ideal nose position. In general, the butt points along a line from the notch between thumb and forefinger to the armpit.

To consistently get the ball in a forward position, the punter should extend but not lock his elbow, point his elbow toward the ground, and place the ball over his punting hip (right hip for a right-footed punter). The punter needs to mold the ball and get it into proper position as soon as he can because that gives him more time to adjust the ball to fit his sight picture.

We often do a molding and presentation drill in which the punters toss snaps to each other and catch, grip, and extend the ball. You can combine this drill with a snapper drill or use a Jugs machine.

Approach

Some punters are most comfortable with two-step approaches and others with three-step approaches. There have been great punters of both types. The only time I insist the punter take two steps is when we are snapping the ball inside our own 5-yard line or when the opponent is in a desperate 11-man-block situation.

The number of steps a punter takes is irrelevant as long as he gets the ball away in a reasonable time and distance. Our standards are 4 yards or less handling distance and less than 1.4 seconds handling time from catch to punt (less than 1.3 seconds during a game on account of adrenaline). Regularly timing the punter's handling does a few important things. First, it helps the punter develop the rhythm and pace he will use in the game. It gives him confidence in his fundamentals. If he is confident, he won't feel the need to change the speed, biomechanics, or timing of his game punts. Second, the data may help you make certain decisions. For example, if 1.4 seconds results in 50-yard punts and 1.2 seconds results in 35-yard punts, you may want to allow your punter more time. Finally, frequent timing will result in greater consistency between practice performance and game performance, a boost in game planning for you and the coverage men.

Given a good snap, the punter should move toward his target with a short jab step (6 to 10 inches). He takes this step either slightly before or immediately after the catch depending on his catching ability and handling time. He should land just outside the midline of his body, as if he were walking a wide balance beam. This often takes practice; don't assume your punter can walk straight.

Punters who wander from side to side often have problems with consistency because even if they are good ball droppers, their bodies aren't in the same place relative to the ball from one punt to another. The most common mistakes made by wandering punters are overstriding or stepping too far outside with the first step. Both detract from consistency and power. Overstriding brakes the forward movement. By placing his support foot too far in front of his center of gravity, the wandering punter ends up with a vaulting, up-and-down movement and slow, jerky approach steps. Stepping too wide makes the punter wander from side to side, just as you would fall over if you lifted one foot while standing with your feet shoulder-width apart. These and other variations disrupt the punter's forward body momentum (weight times speed), which is a large portion of the overall momentum (body plus foot momentum) that he transfers to the ball.

Punters can practice their stepping to improve their technique. It's best to start without a ball. After the main workout, as a warm-up drill, or in a hallway as a study break they can practice short, inward initial steps as well as full approaches that stress handling time and distance. The next level is taking a snap, live or from a Jugs machine, and working down a line to emphasize lateral control (figure 9.8) or down the field to evaluate handling distance.

Figure 9.8 Approach steps down a line.

Drop

Presenting the ball to the foot in a consistent manner is the most important and difficult skill in punting. Consequently, the majority of punt problems start with the drop. The challenge is that a punter has to successfully and repeatedly control the ball front to back, top to bottom, side to side, nose up or down, and nose in or out, so it's impossible to practice this skill enough.

Drop control primarily comes from the shoulder. The movement of too many joints (tossing the ball, pushing the ball, moving the wrist and elbow, and so on) achieves nothing and adds inconsistency to the drop. Once the punter successfully presents the ball and starts his approach, he must slowly guide the ball 6 to 8 inches down a line passing through the punter's hip—the "drop line." Figure 9.9 shows the ball at different points during the drop, passing vertically down the drop line.

The goal of holding onto the ball a bit longer and guiding the ball down the drop line is to slow down the drop, delay the effects of the wind, and establish a path to the best striking position. The longer the punter holds onto the ball and avoids putting the ball in free fall, the greater control he has, the less effect the wind has, and the slower the ball falls to the striking point. Just as it is easier to hit a lob than a fastball, it's easier to hit a slower, guided drop than a swiftly falling one. Guided, delayed drops are more consistent, are struck higher with better hang time, and

Figure 9.9 The drop line.

eliminate the rushed leg swings that result when the ball is lower and faster than anticipated. I ask my guys to imagine putting a sleeping baby in a bassinet or placing eggs in a basket.

Altering the drop plane (nose up or down) doesn't change the mechanics of the drop. The drop is still delayed as the ball is guided 6 to 8 inches down the drop line, but the ball meets the foot a bit lower with the nose down or a bit higher with the nose elevated. Only the initial sight picture at presentation is altered. Any change comes from the shoulder.

The exact position of the ball at foot strike varies from punter to punter and often from punt to punt, but some general principles apply. A punter should hit the ball at the level of his plant-foot knee for a field punt that has good hang time and distance. Lowering the drop plane (angling the nose down slightly) and the contact point to below knee level (figure 9.10) results in a drive punt with more distance than hang time.

A good drill for the drive punt is punting through the goalposts. The punter lines up on the 50-yard line and modifies his drop plane, contact point, and body position to drive the punt through the goalposts. To make this a directional drill, the punter does the same thing from the hash marks. This drill is good for practice competition and change of pace.

The coffin-corner punt is essentially a drive punt at a more extreme angle. A good drill for the coffin-corner punt is working at various field

Figure 9.10 Contact point for the drive punt.

locations to punt the ball out of bounds inside the 20-yard line or at a target just beyond the sideline.

Striking the ball above the knee with an elevated drop plane (nose slightly up) results in a hang or pooch punt with more hang time than distance (figure 9.11). A good drill for perfecting the pooch punt is punting over a light pole. The punter backs up 30 yards and punts the ball over a light pole, modifying his drop plane, contact point, and body position. Another good drill is to snap the ball from the +40-yard line to the −40-yard line and have the punter drop it on the 10-yard line with good hang time.

Figure 9.11 Contact point for the pooch punt.

Regardless of the grip, a lazy finger or thumb on the ball will make the ball rotate, usually unpredictably and with poor results. The punter must release the ball with the simultaneous extension of all fingers. I prefer the ball to appear frozen as it falls to the ground. Eliminate any rotation or torque.

We begin every practice with 10 drops along yard lines or sidelines in each compass direction. We do static drops with the ball in the presentation position, plant foot forward, punting foot back. The punter guides the ball slowly down the drop line and touches the punting thigh with the drop hand after release. A variation is having the punter walk around the field, using the out of bounds lines or track lanes as guides. This emphasizes the most important aspect of punting, the drop, and shows the punters what different wind speeds and directions do to their drops. We progress through the approach steps and drop the ball without swinging at it, taking a snap from the Jugs machine or a snapper and measuring the handling time to ensure punters are operating at game pace. We regularly punt for process instead of focusing on the result. For example, I instruct punters to do five punts with perfect drops, focusing only on the drop and not worrying about the ball's flight.

Leg Swing

A straight-leg swing and flat punting foot at contact are essential if a punter is to be consistent. The leg swing is not just for looks. A straight swing path combined with a consistent drop down the drop line gives the punter the largest window of opportunity to hit a decent punt. A curved swing path reduces the window and makes consistency difficult since few punters can duplicate this curve from repetition to repetition.

Imagine two straight lines, one (the drop line) coming from above and the other (the swing path) coming from below (figure 9.12a). If they are in the same plane, there are many points of intersection at which the ball can be hit. Now imagine a straight drop line intersecting a curved swing path (figure 9.12b). There are very few points of intersection, illustrating why crossover leg swings usually make for inconsistent punts.

The other problem crossover punters have is they must make complex adjustments for drive and hang time punts. Not only do they alter the drop plane, but they must also make left or right drop adjustments to find the right contact points on the swing path.

Correcting a big crossover isn't easy because the punter probably has been kicking soccer balls or field goals much of his life. He gets the sensation that he's punting the ball harder when he crosses over. Unfortunately for him, harder isn't better. It's more important to hit the ball well than it is to hit it hard. A hamstring- and hip-stretching routine combined with an

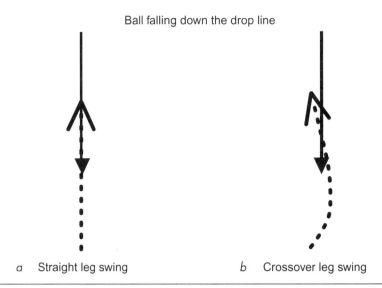

Ball falling down the drop line

a Straight leg swing   *b* Crossover leg swing

Figure 9.12 Leg swing paths: straight leg and crossover leg.

abductor-strengthening program will help his body adjust. Warm-up and cool-down drills emphasizing straight-leg swing will reinforce the correct muscle memory, as will emphasizing straight-leg swing instead of punt results during practice (process versus product).

Going through the approach without a ball and swinging the leg while going down a yard line gives the punter a gauge by which he, a partner, or the coach can assess his swing. He should pick out a point 3 yards in front of him and swing through it. You can observe from the front, noting his flexion (the back part of the swing where the knee is bent) as well as his follow-through. If the punter's foot is cocked back and over the opposite buttock as he flexes, he'll swing out and around the ball, resulting in a crossover. His follow-through should fall between his nose and punting-side ear (figure 9.13).

The final element of a good swing is a plantar-flexed punting ankle with the toe pointed straight so that the foot forms a flat, solid striking surface (see figure 9.10, page 150). Raising the toe can cause shanks. The toe will hit the nose of the ball instead of the top of the foot hitting the ball's sweet spot.

Video from the front is valuable for analyzing and correcting leg swing problems, especially when it shows the player punting down the hash mark or another straight line that you can use as a reference. Again, we punt for process instead of product, asking the punters to punt five with perfect leg swings, including foot position.

Figure 9.13 Straight-leg swing follow-through.

Another excellent drill for developing solid leg swing mechanics is the partner ball pass. Two punters line up about 40 yards apart. Using proper drop technique, straight-leg swing, pointed toes, and upper-body control, they lightly punt the ball or pass it to each another, striving for solid contact and mechanics. After mastering the basic technique, the punters should hold onto the ball so that they are nearly punting the ball out of their hands. This emphasizes holding onto the ball longer and reinforces the need for a straight-leg swing when executing pooch or hang punts.

Plant-Leg Drive

The punter must be able to drive off the ground and up and through the ball using powerful plant-leg knee and hip extension (figure 9.14).

Strong, well-timed drive is one of the most important factors in high, far punts. Often punters do little or nothing with their plant leg or they delay the push off the ground until after punting the ball. Dry-run punts with small plyometric hurdles set approximately one foot in front of the

Figure 9.14 Plant leg driving the punter upward and downfield.

plant-foot position will force the punter to drive up and forward with his plant leg, thus developing that movement sequence. Holding onto the ball 0.1 second longer during the drop, something most punters need to do anyway, will delay ball strike so that it coincides with the plant-leg drive.

Body Position

Approximately 70 percent of a player's body mass is above his waist, so what the punter does with his head and shoulders has a profound effect on the punt's consistency, height, and distance. Maintaining slight forward lean—the athletic position—throughout the approach and the punt will carry the punter down the field, adding body momentum to that of the foot striking the ball. Driving through the ball and down the field rather than trying to hit the ball harder increases the punt's power and distance, allowing the punter to swing with maximum coordination, control, and consistency. A slightly exaggerated athletic posture along with a lower drop plane and contact point results in a drive punt with more distance than hang time. Figure 9.15 shows a good drop plane and contact point for a drive punt, but I'd prefer the body to lean a bit more forward. This is a great punt to hit into a headwind, over a returner's head, or when deep in your own territory.

Forward lean also reduces the effort needed to move forward in the initial stages of the approach, and less effort usually results in greater consistency. An exaggerated forward lean—hunching over the ball as

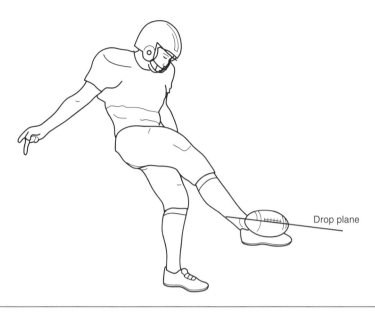

Drop plane

Figure 9.15 Drop plane and contact point of the drive punt.

figure 9.16 illustrates—gives the punter the illusion he's following through. In actuality he's adding error to his punt by failing to control his center of gravity. He's slowing down his leg by quickly reducing his hip angle beyond the maximum power range. Don't let your punters hunch over the ball.

A more upright posture at the contact point causes the punter to drive more upward. Combined with an elevated drop plane and contact point, the result is a punt with greater hang time than distance. This type of punt is excellent for forcing fair catches and pooching inside the 20. Figures 9.11 (page 150) and 9.16b show proper adjustment of the contact point and drop plane, although the punter in figure 9.16b should be more upright for a hang or pooch punt.

Leaning backward increases shanks and inconsistency. Don't let your punters fall backward. A good drill for correcting too much backward lean is walking behind and to the side of your punter through his approach, placing your hand on his back. Keep your hand in the same position, and as the punter leans backward, he'll feel your hand pressing on his back.

From left to right (front view), maintaining body control is also important for accuracy and consistency. The shoulders and hips should be squared and perpendicular to the desired punt line. If the punter dips his shoulders, moves his hips up and down excessively, or falls off to the side during the follow-through, he'll be inconsistent because his foot always ends up in a different position relative to the drop, even if he's an outstanding ball dropper. Smooth, consistent movements are what you're after.

Figure 9.16 Variations in body position and drop plane for executing (a) a field punt and (b) a hang or pooch punt.

We do a "drive and glide" drill to emphasize postural control. The objective is to swing straight through, pressing the punting thigh against the chest for an exaggerated period, while driving forward 1 yard down a line, using the plant leg for thrust and the torso for directional control. When you watch from the side, you can assess the punter's forward progress. From the front you can check for side-to-side movements. This is a good drill for cooling down or adding repetitions without actually punting the ball and wearing out the punter's leg. As with the drop or leg swing, we do five punts for drive only, concentrating on the process, not the product.

Mental Mastery

Punting is 80 percent effort—timing, coordination, rhythm, and control are more important than raw power. I urge my guys to play golf because the mental aspects of golf parallel those of punting. Players must be relaxed to be consistent. If the punter tries to hit the ball too hard, giving the old 110 percent, he'll perform worse. Consequently, most punters don't respond well to the "try harder" vein of coaching advice. That's not to say that they don't need to work hard, but usually relaxation and technique advice work best. Know your punter and what types of encouragement he responds to.

There are three mental levels of punting: *ignorance*, in which a player's just whacking away at balls and doesn't have much of a clue what he's doing; *understanding,* in which he knows what to do, why to do it, and understands what happens when something goes wrong; and *command,* in which he develops the mental toughness and control to direct his body and mind to do what is necessary to get the job done. At the command level, the punter knows that concentration doesn't mean gritting his teeth and squinting; it means he adjusts for conditions and makes the few essential things happen. His mind is a weapon.

Great punters have to be both technician and artist. The technician must understand the biomechanics, physics, and techniques involved in punting; his common errors; and what he must fix in order to improve. He has to have organized practices, and he must record process and performance data in an organized way in order to study, analyze, and correct. The artist enjoys (or at least tolerates) the monotony, toil, and drudgery inherent in the thousands of repetitions. He understands that few people in the world can do what he does, and he appreciates the gifts and opportunities he's been given. He demands excellence, understanding that perfection is only in the mind. Finally, he sees a well-hit punt for what it is, simultaneously a fleeting thing of beauty and a potentially lethal arrow aimed at the heart of a worthy opponent.

Wind Adjustments

Most right-footed punters prefer to punt with a slight left-to-right crosswind because it places the ball over the right hip more consistently, cancels out some hooks, and helps the slightly slicing line drive. The opposite is true for a right-to-left wind. It tends to drift the drop toward the punter's midline, which often makes him hook the ball to his left.

Tailwinds don't affect the drop as much as crosswinds because the punter's body somewhat shields the ball. The punt tends to go farther and flatter, and the nose often does not turn over. A punter needs to hit a hang-time punt with a wind at his back to counter these effects.

Headwinds are tough in that they exaggerate flaws in every aspect of a punter's stroke. If he drops the ball with the nose too far in or he doesn't hold onto the ball long enough, he may hit the ball perpendicular to his foot, most likely resulting in a shank or other end-over-end punt. A slightly off-center hit may look promising at first, then flutter like a wounded bird. If the punter doesn't present and guide the ball far enough in front, he'll drop the ball too close to his body and hook it or hit it on his shin. Headwinds expose poor or mediocre punters, which is why you should have your men punt into the wind as often as possible during practice. The punter absolutely must hold onto the ball longer in the drop to keep control and lessen the wind's effect. He must overemphasize the ball-over-hip position. He should drop a bit of grass at the presentation point (arm extended, chest-height, over right hip) to get a feel for what the wind will do to his drop.

Evaluation

You must have a stopwatch or wristwatch with lap-timing capability, clipboard, paper, and pencil. With these things you can time the snap, handling time, and hang time; record relevant data such as punt distance, return yards, field position, and wind; and analyze the information.

Raising the technical bar a bit, you need good video feedback to assess and improve form. Most practice and game video, shot from the end zone or sideline, is too far away to be of much value. Close-up views from the front and side give the punter feedback on every aspect of punting. At a minimum, a camcorder is adequate, but the capture rate of 30 frames per second (30 Hz) makes viewing ball–foot contact more difficult.

A better option is an SVHS, high-end beta, or digital video camera. These are 60-Hz formats, and your chances of capturing the point of interest are twice as good. When shooting video, it's critical to adjust the shutter to 500 or better; otherwise, the leg swing will be a useless blur. Adjusting the shutter to 500+ makes each frame crisp and distinct. A stop-action VCR is an important tool for before- or after-practice meetings. I'm fortunate to have access to a laptop and Dart Trainer software that, combined with a digital video camera, gives us immediate, on-field feedback after every punt.

I don't chart the punters every day because I believe they need time to experiment with technique. Constant evaluation and competition makes guys conservative and unwilling to try new things, which inhibits growth and improvement. I usually chart punts one day per week during the season and double that in preseason or spring ball. I record line of scrimmage, hash mark, protection call (we are a directional punting team), handling time, handling distance, punt distance and hang time, where the ball hits, and whether or not it was a good spiral (ball is parallel to the ground at the maximum height of the punt).

I load those results into a spreadsheet to track trends, look at competition, and so on. I multiply the punt distance by 10 times the hang time (to make hang time and distance equivalent), resulting in a big number (for example, a 40-yard punt with a hang time of 4.0 seconds would be worth 1,600). This large number allows me to better discriminate between the competing punters. I also multiply the handling time by the distance, and if that product is greater than 5.6 (1.4 seconds × 4 yards), the punter receives a zero for that punt. The underlying thought is if he's too long or too slow, the punt could get blocked, so he shouldn't be rewarded for a substandard punt. I also calculate and keep the raw number to see if any trends develop. Finally, I track all information on game punts.

Tackling

The opposing punt returner is usually the most agile athlete on the field, so punters need to be able to tackle at least well enough that they don't get hurt. They should do defensive back tackling drills, angle tackling, open field tackling, and participate in some team tackling drills, emphasizing form. They must understand the absolute necessity of getting a superior athlete on the ground in whatever way possible.

Conditioning

Our punters participate in the same year-round strength and conditioning program as the defensive backs, doing the same weight program, speed development, pattern runs, and plyometrics. I place greater emphasis on flexibility, warming up, and abdominal (core) strength, but otherwise the program is the same. If the punters work with the defensive backs, they'll not only be challenged by great athletes working on similar skills and thought patterns, but through their work ethic, they'll show the other players on the team that they are true football players, committed to individual excellence and helping their teammates achieve their goals. Greater teamwork, camaraderie, and success grow from working with their teammates, and we avoid developing a distinction between the punters and the other position players on the team.

I don't think it's necessary to punt 100 balls a day. A tired leg is an uncoordinated leg, and it's difficult to focus on that many punts in a session. I prefer 20 to 40 punts three times a week in the off-season. We punt that amount on Tuesday and Wednesday during the season, 10 to 15 on Monday and Thursday, and none on Friday or Sunday. I discourage punting a bunch into the net on game day—players punt just enough to stay loose and focused. Pregame warm-up also should be just enough to get loose. I ask punters to do some work throughout the year to keep up with their bodies as they get bigger, faster, and stronger.

Punting is best learned with the KISS (Keep It Simple) principle, but it is by no means easy. Successful punting requires a blend of athleticism, work ethic, mental toughness, commitment, coaching, and quality teammates, and it can be difficult to get all those things in the same athlete at the same time. Important skills include catching, presenting, and dropping the ball; taking the correct approach steps; performing proper leg swing; and driving through the ball with the plant leg using the right body position. Drills that isolate these skills help punters and coaches perfect individual elements and solve problems observed during full-blown punting. Focusing on the process by concentrating on one skill at a time eventually results in the product you want: consistently outstanding performance.

CHAPTER 10

© Human Kinetics

KICKING OFF

JOE ROBINSON

University of Arizona

Kickoff coverage is one of the most important aspects of special teams performance. As a coordinator, the two things I want to do each week are ensure our own punt and field goal protection and control our opponent's return game. The two most important statistics in every football game are turnovers and field position. Kickoff coverage and the kicker's strategies and ability have a huge effect on field position.

Like every other player on the team, the kicker needs your help. You do not need to be a kicking guru since most kickers have already developed a style and have attended camps with different kicking instructors, but you still need to talk with the kicker and film him in an individual session. Find the things that have made him successful and uncover the mistakes or inconsistencies in his performance. Take the time to consult with his summer instructors. Watch for the good and the bad and give him feedback to help him become more consistent.

Most coaches go through the kicking period of practice and then send the kickers to another field to get better. We would never consider this approach for quarterbacks or linebackers, but this is a common strategy when it comes to specialists. As we will see, there are specific strategies for approaching deep kicks and the practice session that help the overall performance of special teams.

Finally, keep in mind that there are a number of ways to cover the field. Work hard to identify the strengths of your kickoff specialist and then look at your options for coverage. We all look for distance and then for hang time and proper placement. Find out what your kicker brings to the table and then work within those strengths to make your coverage the best it can be.

Individual Kickoff Techniques

If you look at kicking off and the different styles that kickers use, it is easy to see that there are a number of alignments, steps, and styles that are all effective. At Arizona we have the luxury of recruiting kickers, so we look for results and ability and then we work within the framework of the kicker's style. We do not spend as much time on development as we do on building skills and working on consistency. I highly recommend this approach if you are fortunate enough to have an experienced kicker. Through film study and drills simply reinforce the things that have made this individual successful, and always work for consistency.

If you do not have the luxury of a trained kicker, there are some specific fundamentals that you should stress as you begin to build your kicker's technique. Don't allow your kicker to think that there is only one way to do things. Each kicker will eventually develop his unique style, but the following outline will give your kicker a place to start.

Steps and Alignment

The entire kickoff is six and a half steps, building from a jab step to a burst. To find an initial alignment, the kicker can begin at the kicking tee and then go through the kicking motion away from the tee at an angle he believes to be appropriate for the start. This should help him find a place to begin the trial-and-error process of finding the perfect starting position. Not counting the initial jab step, the sixth step is the placement of the plant foot. Once the kicker runs through the motion a few times and feels comfortable with the steps, he should have a good idea of the start position.

The kicker should mark this starting point and then line up on the tee. He should take comfortable steps backward until he has reached correct depth for the starting point. These steps need to be consistent, so they should be as close as possible to a normal walk even though he is walking backward. Once he reaches the correct depth, he should turn and walk over to the beginning point that he previously marked (figure 10.1).

Figure 10.1 Kicker at the proper angle and depth from the tee.

Most kickers are comfortable with about four lateral steps to their alignment. Our current kicker at the University of Arizona takes 10 walking steps away from the 35-yard line, which gives him a depth of 9 yards. He then takes 4 1/2 lateral steps to the left to hit his starting point. Some kickers feel that additional width helps them better use their lower body to create more power.

Approach

The kicker should get into alignment, aiming for the spot where his plant foot will land. He should begin with a jab step and then build up tempo until the last three steps are at a fast pace. Your kicker will figure out how he wants to place the plant foot. Our current kicker likes the plant foot to land at the midpoint of the block, about one foot's length away from the tee (figure 10.2). Wherever he is comfortable is fine; it is consistency that matters. Consistency of the plant foot is one of the most important parts of the entire process.

Figure 10.2 The plant foot lands about a foot away from the tee at the midpoint.

Contact

The first thing to look for at contact is leg and ankle lock with the toes pointed down (figure 10.3). Leg lock and leg speed produce the strike on the ball. If the kicker is losing some of his drive, look back on film for the lock point to see where he's going wrong. The lock is produced by driving the knee with great speed and then snapping the leg out with emphasis on the lock. The arms should be relaxed and natural.

Figure 10.3   The leg and ankle lock with the toes pointing down.

The follow-through is a powerful motion (figure 10.4). After contact, the kicker lands on his kicking foot. To achieve proper follow-through, have the kicker imagine that he is jumping over a hurdle from the point of contact until the landing. This creates lift for the follow-through and helps pull the legs and hips through the kick.

Figure 10.4 Powerful follow-through with hurdling motion.

Results

We look for kicks into the end zone with hang times of 4 seconds or more. These results indicate a kicker with a great deal of ability. If the kicker is unable to reach the end zone, focus on lengthening hang time and working on placement to help the coverage unit.

Specialty Kicks

We ask kickers to work on specialty kicks that we may need at different points during the season, specifically the squib kick and the sky kick.

Kickers change very little for squib kicks. The steps, alignment, and approach are the same. The kicker aims for the middle of the football and cuts down a bit on the follow-through. He should feel as if he is driving down on the football.

For sky kicks, the ultimate advantage is showing the same alignment and approach. When most players try this kick, they round off the end of the approach. Have the kicker point the tee at the target area, which for us is between the 22- and 28-yard lines. At contact, the kicker stays on his plant foot and skips through the kick, much like the motion for a field goal. He leans back for additional height and swings through at less than full speed. Some kickers are more successful when they use their field goal alignment and approach, which is the correct approach if it produces results. For the return unit, the sky kick makes the prekick read difficult, a big advantage for the kicking team.

Deep Kicks

Obviously the deep kick is the kickoff of choice for most teams most of the time. Cover the entire field by opening up the target area for the kicker or cover only a portion of the field by asking the kicker to pin the ball in a smaller target area. As you make this decision for your team, consider the following:

- Does either kick present a problem and if so, why?
- How much effect will placing the ball have on the kicker?
- Are we willing to accept a penalty if we ask the kicker to pin the ball in the corner and we get one out of bounds?
- Is the kicker a distance kicker or a hang-time kicker?
- Looking at the games we have to win this season, what strategy will work best against these teams?

I prefer to use a corner kick. We train our kickers by giving them a specific target area during practice. We form a 10-yard square using cones. We place two cones on the goal line, one 5 yards from the boundary and one 5 yards outside the hash mark. (The college hash mark is currently 20 yards from the boundary.) We place two cones on the 10-yard line, one 5 yards from the boundary and one 5 yards outside the hash mark. This gives the kicker his target area. We want balls to land in the target area or go over the target area into the end zone. For this type of kick, you want a 4.0-second hang time to allow for maximum coverage.

Decisions about kick direction are simply a matter of trial and error. My experience is that the direction of the kick (left or right corner) can make a huge difference to the kicker. The direction of the kick has never seemed to affect the coverage. Most of the kickers I have worked with have preferred to come across their bodies. Right-footed kickers seem to like the left corner. For this type of kick, most kickers need to place the ball on or close to the hash mark nearest their target.

From a coverage standpoint, I like to cover two-thirds of the field with two safeties (one lane runner and the kicker), two contain players, and seven lane runners.

A player who can consistently place the ball in either corner from the middle of the field is an exceptional kicker who can create a huge advantage for your team in terms of your overall hit chart. In that case, you must look at coverage. When they kick the ball into the corner, some teams flip their coverage personnel based on the direction of the kick. This gives away a little of their advantage. I recommend working out a mirror scheme so that the direction of the kick surprises the return team.

If your kicker can consistently drive the ball into the end zone but is bothered by corner placement, you need to cover the field to give him the best chance for success. I would do this only if the percentage of end zone kicks is very high, well over 50 percent. Play kicks in this scheme give the kickoff return unit a greater chance for success.

I have had the opportunity to work with kickers with strong legs who fought the idea of the corner kick. In time, however, they mastered the target and still managed to drive the football. Experience has taught me that you can get the best of both worlds. Ask the kicker to continue to drive the ball but work toward the target and on increased hang time. Chart each kick for placement and hang time. Effort and attention in this area will create a kicker who can drive the ball into the end zone but also can provide a better kick to cover when the ball is in play.

Sky Kicks

The sky, or pooch, kick is a crucial part of the kickoff package. At times you just do not want to put the ball in the hands of a great opposing player. We all are confident in our ability to cover kicks, and we like to say that we will accept the challenge of any returner. If need be, that is exactly what we will do. However, the ultimate goal is to win, and sometimes there are better strategies for accomplishing that goal.

I look at a sky kick when faced with the following situations:

- Kicking into a strong wind
- Kicking off in the fourth quarter with a lead, especially if the defense has had a great day and we believe that the opponent's ability to drive the field is limited
- Going against a great returner or return team

When practicing placement of the sky kick, we set up cones to create a target for the kicker, just as we do for corner kicks. We place two cones on the 22-yard line, one 2 yards from the boundary and the other 8 yards from the boundary. We place cones on the same landmarks on the 28-yard line, giving us a target area that is 6 yards square. If you can get a 4.0-second hang time to this target, you will make any return very tough for your opponent.

We try to use the same coverage lanes as in our corner kick scheme. Obviously our players are aware of the new target area and must adjust their personal zones as they cover the field. Watch that the coverage players do not try to squeeze the field too soon. The most dangerous returns off sky kicks seem to be back across the field.

This is our philosophy on sky kicks: If we force our opponent to start on the 20-yard line, we have been successful. Touchbacks and coverage units that can tackle at the 20 or better are why we work kickoff coverage. But even a strong kicker will not get a touchback when kicking into a good wind. If he executes the kick properly, there is a great chance for a fair catch somewhere between the 22- and the 28-yard line. If the coverage is good, we feel that we can hold any return to a minimum. This kick should be part of your overall scheme, especially when you consider how few yards you give up if the kick is properly executed. In addition, it will help you to build a complicated hit chart.

Squib Kicks

The squib kick can also be a great complement to the overall package. A lot of coaches like to look at the squib kick in the same situations I listed for the sky kick. I prefer to stay with the sky kick in those situations, saving the squib kick for very late in the half or game. I look at the squib kick not so much from a position standpoint, as with the sky kick, but from a contain standpoint, as you would want when kicking off with 5 seconds left in the half.

Similar to the deep kick, most kickers are going to want to have the entire field to kick the squib. We work with our kickers on kicking the squib in the direction of the corner kick target, being cautious, however, of not flirting with going out of bounds. For that reason, you have to concentrate on the integrity of your coverage lanes. If you use a field coverage scheme with a corner kick, use that coverage with the squib kick as well.

With the squib kick, you want to ensure that the players relax on the play and contain concerns. You will probably see an uncoordinated return, but the returner usually has space, and this is a time when laterals and throwbacks are always a concern. You and your players should discuss and practice squib kick situations.

Kickers at Practice

All specialists need to have focus and direction during practice. Too often coaches send the kickers to another field during the bulk of the practice session and tell them to get better. We would never consider doing this with linebackers or quarterbacks because we know that the focus and direction we give them in practice helps them to be their best. Kickers are not any different. Just like any other position, you can coach kickers and you can see the same improvement.

During the time before practice, we prepare for the practice session as if it were a game. Our kickers go through the drills they use to prepare for field goals and kickoffs. We use a field goal progression of no-step kicks, one-step kicks, two-step kicks, and full field goals. The full kicks move from hash mark to hash mark and yard line to yard line. We work a goalpost drill for trajectory. For kickoffs, kickers again build up to the full kick by warming up with a short approach. They also work approaches on air to time out their steps.

A real key for kickers is to not overkick during this time, just as they would not overkick to prepare for a game. Communication is vital. Talk to the kickers and observe their performance. Use the warm-up period to observe your kickers and figure out how they will fit into the game plan. This entire session should be about 15 minutes long.

Most practice sessions involve a team stretch and some kicking. Kickers execute their responsibilities with the rest of the team during this time. One important factor is what you do with the kickers during the rest of the practice session. We take the first 10 minutes of the practice session and work an additional stretch. The team stretch is not enough for the specialists, and kickers will usually ignore stretching if given a chance. Increased flexibility has been a big part of the success of kickers I have known. After the stretch, we take a 30-minute drill period. During pre-practice meetings, we talk to the specialists about the skills they need to improve, and then we give them drills to work those specific areas. This is the same thing that any other position coach would do for his players. If you have enough personnel, have the kickers work together in groups. I move around the field as players drill and talk to them about how the drill is helping their overall game.

We then move to progressions, the time for kickers to perform under pressure and compete head to head. Kickers work a kickoff progression, kicking three kicks to their corner target areas. We chart the results, including placement and hang time. We work a similar three-kick progression for sky kicks and another three-kick progression for onside kicks. We work a three- to five-kick field goal progression, charting operation time along with results. We spend the rest of the time in this period on progressions for punters and snappers. We end the session with an additional stretch, and then we rejoin the full squad for any postpractice activities or conditioning.

We try to add as many gamelike situations to each session as we can. During the drill period, I like to place a ball at a specific spot on the field and call for a quick field goal. We start a countdown and make the operation unit work under pressure. The daily head-to-head competition of the progressions also puts pressure on the kickers. If the backups are not working with a coach during the practice session, they feel they do not have much of a chance to work up the depth chart and the starter gets into a comfort zone that may keep him from improving. By competing on a daily basis, anyone can prove he deserves the chance to win a job. We keep the progressions to a minimum to make each kick more important. I want the kicker to know that he only has three kicks and each of them had better be well executed.

Kickoffs After Safeties and Penalties

A few other situations can arise that you need to prepare for. You may have to kick off from the 20-yard line or the 50-yard line or any yard line in between.

When kicking off from the 50-yard line, most teams prefer to drive the ball through the end zone and start on defense at the 20-yard line. This is a great, safe option. Another option is the sky kick. Our original sky target, as mentioned earlier, is the 22- to the 28-yard line. Taking into account the 15-yard difference, we shoot for the 7- to 13-yard line, again with a target area of 2 to 8 yards from the boundary. This is a little more aggressive approach since it requires good coverage and placement. Most teams, however, are somewhat less disciplined in their return schemes against the sky kick, and the field depth seems to cause even more trouble. Be sure to incorporate this kick during the kicker's individual practice time.

When kicking off from the 20-yard line, most teams use the punter. If you have a kicker with strong legs who gets a lot of touchbacks, take a look at using a long kick. Work all of your schemes within a 65-yard framework, the end zone being the line that you use to set up the timing. The kickoff return team now has an 80-yard framework to work with, yet usually the returner is the only one who adjusts his timing to the added space. You can get an uncoordinated return, and you may be able to buy back some of the yards you lost to the penalty or the safety.

CHAPTER 11

© Paul Chapman/University of Central Florida

KICKING EXTRA POINTS AND FIELD GOALS

BRIAN POLIAN
University of Central Florida

In this chapter we are going to look at how to teach a young player to become a fundamentally sound field goal and extra point kicker. The chapter is written as if we were coaching a right-footed, soccer-style kicker. We'll go through the basic steps of kicking a football, including takeaway, stance, approach, foot-to-ball contact, and leg swing and skip-through. We will also address other key teaching points, such as operation time, plant foot, and the sweet spot.

Keep in mind that the techniques, teaching points, and drills in this chapter are a starting point. Often a kicker has individual quirks, but as long as he can develop a level of consistency in performing the fundamentals, he has a chance for prolonged success.

Kicker's Role

The position of kicker is unique in the game of football for a couple of reasons. First, the kicker has the opportunity to put points on the scoreboard whenever he takes the field. Because of this, he faces a great deal of pressure. The reality of the position is that whenever the kicker takes the field for a field goal or extra point, those points may win or lose the game. Second, the kicker is somewhat isolated. In football—the greatest team game of all—the success or failure of a field goal or extra point often rests on the kicker's shoulders.

Because the position is unique, the coach needs to know how to handle the kicker. I make an effort to remain positive. Instead of telling the player what not to do, I remind him to focus on the positives. For example, instead of saying, "Don't let your plant foot flare out," I'll say, "Keep your plant foot pointed at your target." It sounds silly and small, but coaches should always reinforce positive actions and erase any thought of negative ones. Remind kickers to do the things that help them make the kick, not avoid the things that cause them to miss it.

It is okay to voice some displeasure with the kicker. After all, he is a player who has responsibilities just like his teammates. However, the conversation should end on a positive note, and then the focus must shift to the next play, the only play that the kicker can control.

I often compare swinging a golf club to kicking a football. Every golf swing, although built on basic principles, is unique. That is also true of kicking. Each kicker has some little quirk in his motion or leg swing. I try my best to tweak the fundamentals rather than overhaul the kicker's swing to improve overall performance.

There is also a similarity between swinging a golf club and kicking a football in the sense of routine. Golfers, especially when putting, try to follow a routine for every time they approach a shot. That routine develops muscle memory, helping them execute the action the same way each time. The routine also helps players deal with pressure. When the situation becomes stressful, the players can fall back on the memory and consistency of the routine. Just like a golfer, each kicker should develop a prekick routine.

Another similarity between swinging a golf club and kicking the football is tempo. Tempo is a word we hear a great deal when talking about swinging a golf club or kicking a football. I define tempo as the timing and speed with which the skill is performed. In both movements, you are looking for a consistent and smooth tempo.

Finally, the successful football team practices blocking and tackling around 100 times a year. The successful golfer or kicker practices his skill around 200 times per year. The 200-day player is a mismatch for the 100-day player.

Kicker's Characteristics

Most successful kickers share specific characteristics. These characteristics, both physical and mental, need to be nurtured. For instance, mental toughness, discipline, and attention to detail are mental characteristics that the athlete commits himself to improving. Flexibility and lower-body strength are physical characteristics that the athlete can improve. However these characteristics are developed, they are important for successful, consistent performance.

Mental toughness is a vital trait in a successful kicker. The kicker must be able to concentrate on the task at hand and not be distracted by the environment around him. The kicker must also be able to move on and focus on the next kick after a failure. No kicker will make every kick, but the mentally tough ones have the ability to move past failure and prepare themselves for success at the next opportunity.

Discipline and attention to detail are traits that are necessary for succeeding at anything in life, but they are especially important for kickers for a couple of reasons. With NCAA limits on the number of assistant coaches, the coach who handles the kickers is often also responsible for another position. Because of this, kickers tend to spend a great deal of practice time on their own. It takes a lot of discipline to stay focused on their drills. Kicking also requires attention to detail. Kickers must make sure they are consistently doing the little things right.

A good kicker needs both the lower and upper body to be flexible. Flexible muscles allow for more power at impact, better follow-through, and stable posture throughout the kick. Stretching can be done 365 days a year and takes little time. We often tell kickers to sit on the floor and stretch while they are watching TV. They simply need to make it a habit.

Obviously a kicker who has a great deal of lower-body strength will be able to transfer more power to the ball. Points of emphasis are the quadriceps, hamstrings, gluteals, calves, and muscles in and around the hips. However, the kicker should never trade strength for flexibility. We do not want the kicker to become so muscular that he becomes stiff.

Kicker's Techniques

A kicker who has sound technique will be able to consistently kick the ball well. Although individual kickers will vary somewhat in their techniques, the basics of takeaway and stance, operation time (the time between the snap and the kick), approach and footwork, foot-to-ball-contact, and leg swing and follow-through are vital to every kicker.

Takeaway and Stance

Takeaway refers to the backward steps the kicker takes to get into position to approach the ball. The following description is a starting point; the takeaway can slightly differ depending on the individual player.

The kicker first shows the holder his spot, or where he wants the ball to be placed. He then aligns his plant foot (the nonkicking foot) to the spot. From that point, the kicker takes three normal steps backward (figure 11.1a). After the kicker has moved backward, he takes two normal

Figure 11.1 Takeaway: *(a)* kicker takes three normal steps back from the placement spot; *(b)* he takes two normal steps to the left.

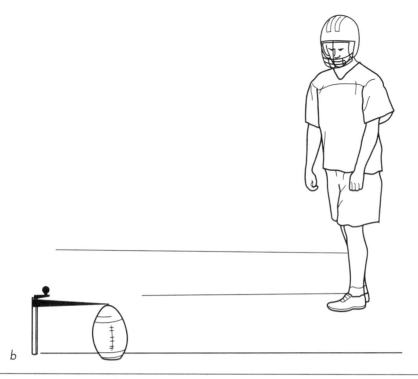

Figure 11.1 *(continued)*

steps to the left (figure 11.1b). I emphasize *normal* because when a kicker's steps are too long or short, they affect how he approaches the football and where his plant foot lands.

Once the kicker has completed his takeaway, he must align himself in the proper stance with his body in good relationship to the target. The kicker's body should lean forward slightly (figure 11.2). He must be ready to react to his key as the ball is snapped. He should not stand erect because it takes more time to get the body moving forward. A good athletic stance with a slight forward lean enables a smooth transition as the kicker approaches the spot on the snap.

The feet should be slightly less than shoulder-width apart and slightly staggered. The plant foot (left foot for a right-footed kicker) should be forward in nothing greater than a heel-to-toe relationship. The kicker's weight should be on the balls of his feet, not the toes. If his body weight is too far forward, it can cause a stutter step or stumble on the approach to the spot.

The arms should be in a comfortable position, either hanging at the sides or slightly out in front. The head should be down, eyes focused on the holder's hand. The waist should be slightly bent so that the shoulders are in front of the hips. Finally, the kicker should be facing and moving

Figure 11.2 Proper stance.

directly toward the target. This is crucial for the kicker to learn: The basic alignment and all motion thereafter move directly toward the target.

Operation Time

Operation time is the amount of time between the snap and the actual kicking of the ball. The longer the operation time, the longer the protection unit has to protect and the more time the opponent has to try to block the kick. The kicker plays a vital role in keeping operation time to a minimum.

In the section about takeaway and stance, I mentioned the spot, or the place on the field where the kicker wants the holder to place the football when he fields the snap. The kicker always aligns in relationship to the spot and the target. The holder places his right hand over the spot and his left hand out in front of it to give the snapper an aiming point. The kicker needs to focus on the holder's right hand because that hand is the kicker's movement trigger. When the holder raises his right hand to field the snap, the kicker begins his approach. If the kicker waits until he sees the ball placed on the spot, it slows the operation time and gives the opponent more time to create pressure. An ideal operation time in college football is 1.25 seconds or less.

Approach and Footwork

The approach to the spot is a series of three steps: jab, step, and plant. The first step, the jab, is taken with the left foot (right-footed kicker). It is a 4- to 6-inch jab step. The kicker is not looking to gain a great deal of ground, only to set the body in motion and create a sense of timing and rhythm to the approach. It is almost as if the kicker picks up the left foot and puts it right back down.

The next step, taken with the kicking foot (right foot for a right-footed kicker), is a stride of normal length and tempo. If a kicker begins to overstride or understride on the second step, it will adversely affect the plant foot and its relationship to the ball.

The third step in the approach is the plant. Successful execution of the plant step is essential to the kick's success. The kicker takes the plant step with the nonkicking foot (left foot for a right-footed kicker). As the plant occurs, the body becomes anchored to the ground as the kicking leg swings around and locks out at the point of contact with the ball. The left leg should have some flex in it when the plant occurs. If the leg is too stiff, it can be difficult to get the ball up in the air quickly.

The plant foot is a key component of a field goal or extra point attempt. The plant foot has a direct effect on the kick's trajectory and relationship to the target. It cannot be said enough—the placement of the plant foot must be consistent.

The ideal plant is 6 to 8 inches to the left of the ball (figure 11.3). That creates enough space for the kicker to get his right leg through at an angle that creates maximal power on impact. If the plant foot is too close to or too far away from the ball, it will be impossible for the kicker to hit

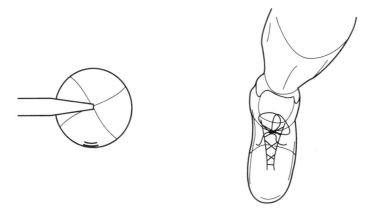

Figure 11.3 The plant foot should be 6 to 8 inches to the left of the ball.

the ball solidly and consistently. Often the placement of the plant foot is to blame for balls that are snap hooks (hard right-to-left movement) or distinct fades (hard left-to-right movement).

As for the depth of the plant foot, the ankle bone should line up with the seam that runs down the side of the ball (figure 11.4). If the kicker is kicking off a tee, the ankle bone can be slightly farther back. If the plant foot gets ahead of the football or too far behind the football, it will be difficult to hit the football in the sweet spot and achieve a solid kick.

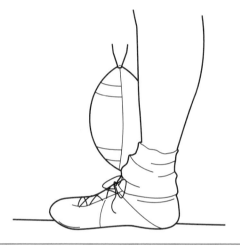

Figure 11.4 The ankle lines up with the seam of the football.

The plant foot's relationship to the target is also a critical point. We always want the plant foot to point directly at the target at impact. It does not point straight, but at the target. When kicking from a hash mark, the target is not straight ahead, it is on an angle. The plant foot needs to guide all of the energy from the kicking leg to the target.

When studying film, note how often the ball's flight follows the path set by the plant foot. The plant foot can force the hips to open too early or stay closed. At the point of impact, the kicker's hips should be square to the target. A consistent plant foot placed square to the target is the first step to keeping the hips square.

Earlier I compared kicking a football and swinging a golf club. The approach and footwork share the most similarities. The kicker needs almost perfect muscle memory every time he approaches the ball. The steps need to be the same length every time. A simple but effective way to check for footwork consistency is to have the kicker kick a handful of balls from the same spot. Look at the grass and make sure that the same places are worn down by the kicker's steps.

The tempo of the approach also needs to be consistent. To borrow a phrase from coach John Wooden, "Be quick, but don't rush." Kickers who have a deliberate and smooth takeaway may still speed through the approach. Operation time is such a concern for some kickers that they actually run at the spot when the ball is snapped. That makes it nearly impossible to have a consistent approach to the football. As long as the kicker begins to move on his key (the movement of the holder's right hand) and his approach is consistent and at a good tempo, operation time should not be an issue.

Foot-to-Ball Contact

The old school of thought, soccer-style kicking, was to use the inside of the foot to strike the football. The part of the foot that struck the ball was just below the big toe, near the inside knuckle of the foot. In the mid-1980s, that teaching began to change. Today the top or middle portion of the foot strikes the football (figure 11.5). In order to achieve contact at this part of the foot, the kicker should point his toes down and out at the moment of impact. Using this portion of the foot enables more surface area to contact the ball, cutting down on the chances of a mis-hit. It also offers a solid bone and cartilage surface that transfers more energy at the moment of impact.

At the moment of impact, the kicking foot should be locked with the toes pointing down and out. The kicking leg should also be locked. There is no flex in the knee and the muscles of the leg are contracted. This locked position enables the transfer of a maximal amount of energy from the kicker's leg to the ball.

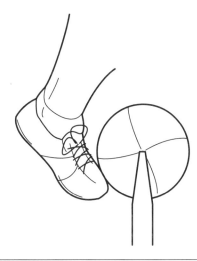

Figure 11.5 The top or middle of the foot strikes the ball.

There is a sweet spot on every football, a place where the maximal amount of energy is transferred to the ball. On most footballs, the sweet spot is approximately 2 inches below the middle. It is a good idea to mark the sweet spot with a marker or paint on the balls kickers use for practice (figure 11.6). To take that teaching tool to the next level, put chalk on the inside of the kicker's shoe. The chalk leaves a mark on the ball that you can compare to the sweet spot. Consistently hitting the sweet spot results in longer, solidly struck kicks.

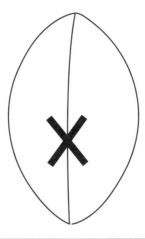

Figure 11.6 Mark the sweet spot on practice balls.

The spin and flight of the football as it comes off the kicker's foot also tells you if the ball was struck on the sweet spot. A well-struck ball comes off the kicker's foot sharply and spins end over end. If the ball has severe overspin and shoots straight into the air, the kicker struck below the sweet spot. If the ball comes off the foot low and knuckles, the kicker struck above the sweet spot. An educated kicker who pays attention to detail should recognize this and easily correct the problem.

Leg Swing and Skip-Through

After the kicker makes solid contact, he must continue the leg swing all the way through the ball (figure 11.7). A good leg swing finishes at least chest high, sometimes even at eye level. Often young kickers have trouble with the leg swing; they want to simply punch at the football. Finishing the leg swing all the way through enables the kicker to drive the football farther, get it into the air quicker, and guide it more easily toward the target. Flexibility is key—flexible hamstrings, quadriceps, and hips allow the leg swing to finish all the way.

Figure 11.7 Complete the leg swing through the football.

The skip-through occurs at the same time as the leg swing. As the kick occurs, the plant foot should skip forward about 6 inches. It is a subtle movement but it ensures that the energy of the kick carries through the football. The skip-through must also move directly toward the target as the kicker drives his body through the football.

The upper body remains relatively quiet throughout the kicking motion. The most important point of emphasis is the front shoulder (left shoulder for right-footed kicker). The kicker must force himself to keep the front shoulder in. When the front shoulder flares out past a point where it is no longer parallel, it forces the front hip to open. When the front shoulder and hip open too early, it makes it impossible for the kicker to be square at the point of impact, and often the ball hooks to the left.

The other point of emphasis for the upper body is the head. The kicker should keep his head down until after he has finished the leg swing and skip-through. Telling him to pin the chin on the chest is an effective way to reinforce this coaching point. By forcing the head to stay down, the kicker can more successfully drive through the ball and finish the kick. Young kickers often want to peek to see the result of the kick before they finish the motion. We often tell our guys, "Stay down on it, and we'll tell you if the kick is good."

Targets

When a kicker aligns himself, he must adjust according to the target. We often have seen young kickers align themselves in the same manner no matter where the ball is placed. Then they try to compensate through the approach to the ball and the leg swing. This is especially troublesome when the ball is placed on a hash mark.

When the kicker sets himself to begin his takeaway, the plant foot and the hips should point at the target. As he sets himself in relationship to the target, the approach, leg swing, and skip-through should be no different than they were 100 times before. Once the kicker is in a good line with the uprights, the kick becomes muscle memory, exactly what we are trying to create.

When it comes to aiming the football, each kicker will get a feel for how the ball moves. When the kicker has that feel, he knows where to aim the ball to give himself the most space between the uprights. For instance, a kicker who hits a ball that has a slight hook (meaning it moves from right to left) wants to aim a few feet right of center. Then the ball will hook through the center of the uprights and leave some room for error on either side. Once a player can hit the ball solidly and gets a feel for how it moves, he can adjust his aiming point accordingly.

Field Goal and Extra Point Drills

Fundamentals are parts of movements that can be practiced individually. The idea is to practice the simple parts of complex movements and then put the pieces together in one complete movement. Many drills can improve the basic fundamentals and in turn the overall kicking of a field goal or extra point.

Thud Drill

The thud drill emphasizes the contact point between the kicking foot and the football. A kicker and holder are needed for the drill. The holder sets the ball down on the spot and applies pressure to the top of the ball. The kicker aligns his plant foot and then takes a half-speed swing at the ball. The ball should not move off the spot (figure 11.8). Check the kicker's foot to make sure that the toes point down and out. Evaluate whether or not the kicker strikes the ball with the correct part

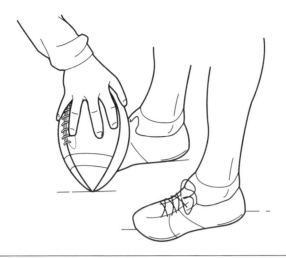

Figure 11.8 Thud drill.

of his foot (the top or middle) and whether or not he strikes the sweet spot on the ball.

Skip-Through Drill

The skip-through drill is a footwork drill that the kicker can do alone. The drill does not involve a football. The kicker simply goes through the takeaway, approach, leg swing, and skip-through on air. The emphasis is on the plant foot's 6-inch skip as the kicker finishes the leg swing. The drill is most effective when the kicker is aligned with a target because we can make sure that the approach, leg swing, and skip-through move toward the uprights.

Leg Swings

Leg swings are a valuable teaching tool as well as a good way to warm up the kicker's leg. The emphasis is on an exaggerated leg swing and correct upper-body posture. The kicker can use the portable holder for this drill. He begins by aligning his plant foot with the ball (figure 11.9). He then takes a full leg swing at the ball. The swing should be exaggerated with a finish as high as possible. Also look at the kicker's front shoulder to make sure he does not flare it out past parallel. If the drill is done correctly, the ball will go only 7 to 10 yards but it will get up quickly and come out end over end.

Figure 11.9 Leg swing drill.

One-Step Drill

The one-step drill is similar to the leg swing drill in that the kicker works on his leg swing and upper-body posture. This drill adds the plant step to the equation. To begin, the kicker takes one step back from the ball and half a step to his left (figure 11.10). From this position, he takes one step (the plant step) and then swings through the football. Emphasize the placement of the plant foot in relation to the football, both width and depth. Also make sure that the plant foot points directly at the target. If the drill is done correctly, the ball will travel only 12 to 15 yards, but it will get up quickly and come out end over end.

Short Shot Drill

The short shot drill is the first drill of the progression in which the kicker puts together the takeaway, approach, leg swing, and skip-through. The ball is placed 2 yards inside the goal line (figure 11.11). The emphasis of the drill is sound fundamentals. Because the kicker is so close to the crossbar, he must ensure that the ball gets good trajectory as it comes off his foot. Flexing the plant leg and hitting the sweet spot are the keys to getting the ball up quickly.

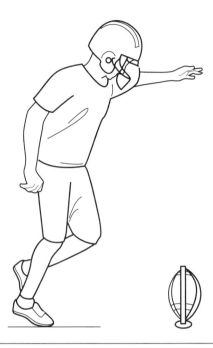

Figure 11.10 One-step drill: Kicker begins one step back and half a step to the left from the ball.

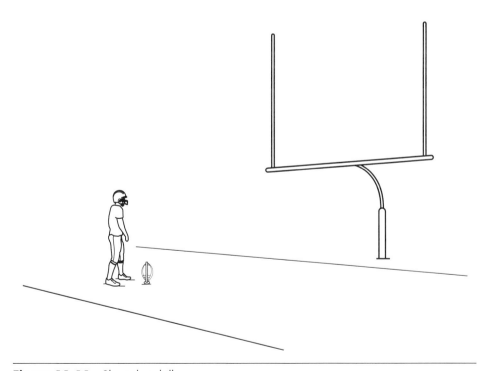

Figure 11.11 Short shot drill.

End-line Accuracy Drill

The end-line accuracy drill is exactly that, a drill that tests the kicker's accuracy. The ball is placed on the end line in the back of the end zone (figure 11.12). From this spot, the kicker kicks the ball across the field. The goal is to hit the ball so that it flies directly over the goalpost or strikes it. An accurate kick is within two feet of either side of the goalpost. The end line serves as a reference to make sure the kicker's plant foot and skip-through are square to the target. This also is a great drill to use as a competition between the kickers.

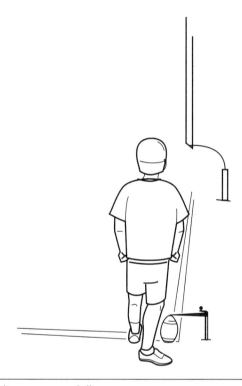

Figure 11.12 End-line accuracy drill.

Hard Angle Drill

The hard angle drill is another drill in which the kicker goes through the entire motion, but the drill shrinks the kicker's target area. The ball is placed well outside the hash mark, shrinking the amount of space between the uprights (figure 11.13). The kicker aligns himself with the much smaller target area and concentrates on being accurate within that small space. This is also a great drill for creating competition among the kickers.

Figure 11.13 Hard angle drill.

These drills and many more like them are helpful for isolating certain movements and emphasizing specific coaching points. Early in the preseason, it is a good idea to teach and reteach every drill to the kickers. Kickers often spend practice time alone, and coaches need to reinforce exactly what fundamentals kickers should work on with each drill.

Another great resource for coaching kickers is videotape. The best film is shot at ground level from behind, from the side, and in front of the kicker. Being able to evaluate themselves on film is a key to the learning process for kickers. Coach Jim Hofher of the University at Buffalo once said, "Inspect, don't expect." Instead of looking at the tape and expecting the player to know what he is doing wrong, ask him to evaluate what he sees. You will gain valuable insight into his level of understanding.

Finally, create as much competition as you can in practice. It keeps the kickers interested in what they are doing, and it creates more gamelike situations. Throw a field goal attempt into the middle of practice with the whole team looking on. That is a real situation kickers will face. It is a pressure-filled kick and there is only one chance for success.

Kickers are in a unique position that takes unique skills. But these skills are no different than any others in the sense that they can be practiced over and over. I hope that I have been able to break down the basic fundamentals of field goal and extra point kicking to show how each is important to the kicker's overall success.

Teaching a player to kick is no different than teaching a student history. There is always a learning process. Tell the player what you want, show him what you want, let him walk through what you want, and if possible, film him doing it and make corrections using the film.

As coaches, remember to stay positive. Sometimes it is just a matter of word choice and delivery. Do not focus on the things that cause failure; instead emphasize the things that bring success.

CHAPTER 12

© Purdue University

LONG SNAPPING

BILL LEGG

Purdue University

Players learn to long snap years before they realize it. They start in backyards, streets, and playgrounds across the country by playing catch with their parents and friends. They lay a foundation not only for throwing the ball but also snapping it. Usually a kid who has learned to throw the ball well but is not a quarterback candidate has the best chance to become a long snapper. The fundamental of throwing the football is a great place to start when trying to find and develop a snapper.

Hands

Hand placement starts out the same as when a quarterback throws a pass. The throwing hand is near the back point of the ball with the fingers spread across the seam that contains the laces (figure 12.1). Hand size determines how many fingers actually overlap the laces. The larger the hand, the more fingers contact the laces.

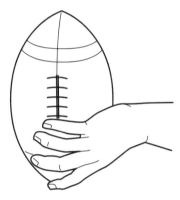

Figure 12.1   Hand near the back of the ball with fingers spread.

The thumb on the throwing hand extends and wraps around to the underside of the ball (figure 12.2). Again, the size of the hand determines how far the thumb extends around the ball.

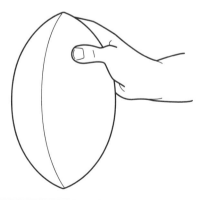

Figure 12.2   The thumb wraps around to the underside of the ball.

After checking the placement of the throwing hand, have the snapper warm up by playing catch with a partner. The focus is on the release of the ball. Like a quarterback's throw, the ball should leave the index finger last in order to maximize rotation and velocity. The rotation must be tight and the ball on target. The snapper's follow-through should be no different from a quarterback's follow-through—down and across to the far hip.

Once the snapper is comfortable with the grip and release, it's time to learn to use the off hand. The off hand is simply a tool for controlling the accuracy of the snap. The concept is similar to that of the off hand in shooting a basketball. Some people refer to the off hand as the guide hand. Before placing the guide hand on the ball, the snapper first needs to slightly rotate or cock the wrist of the throwing hand approximately one-quarter turn (figure 12.3). Then the snapper lays the guide hand on the middle of the underside of the ball. Using the seam opposite the threads as a guide, the snapper runs the middle finger of the guide hand down the seam with the fingers slightly spread but relaxed and pointing toward the back tip (figure 12.4).

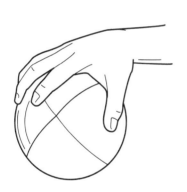

Figure 12.3 Snapper slightly rotates the wrist of the throwing hand.

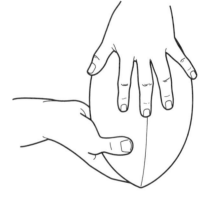

Figure 12.4 The middle finger of the guide hand is on the seam and the fingers are spread.

At this point many snappers begin to have problems with the release, usually because they use too strong of a grip with the guide hand. Snappers must understand that the guide hand simply lies on the ball, exerting only enough pressure to maintain contact with the ball throughout the motion.

A drill for emphasizing this point is the two-hand overhead pass. Players should perform the drill without shoulder pads or helmet to allow both arms to extend fully and comfortably over the head. The snapper stands and throws the ball over his head, playing catch with his partner while making sure that the guide hand stays on the ball to the point of release. Both hands release at the same time, finishing down and away toward the near hip. Players can step toward the target for a more natural feel. Work to improve this motion while still concentrating on rotation and velocity. It is equally important that the rotation remains tight and the pass is on target.

Base

In long snapping, as in every athletic endeavor, the base is the foundation for success. Base width varies with each snapper and each type of snap. Once again the size of the snapper plays a part.

For a punt, the base is formed with the snapper's feet approximately shoulder-width apart and the toes pointing straight ahead (figure 12.5a). This helps the snapper use his legs to increase the snap's velocity. In addition, in today's punt protection schemes in which the snapper helps with the protection as well as the snap, the snapper is able to set easier to his responsibility. Snappers can adjust the base in or out to create the best position for them.

The snapper needs to adjust the base on a short snap for a field goal or extra point. The base needs to be wider to create more stability since the snapper is not moving his feet but holding his ground (figure 12.5b). An added benefit of a wider base on a short snap is it reduces the effect of the legs on the snap, allowing the upper body and arms to remain consistent on both long and short snaps.

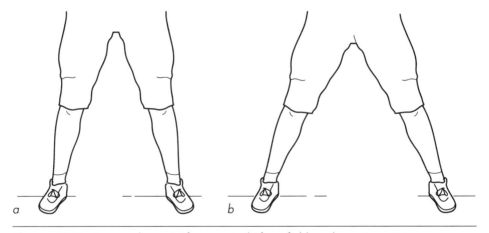

Figure 12.5 Snapper base: *(a)* for a punt; *(b)* for a field goal or extra point.

Body

Positioning the body once the base is set is like loading a spring. If positioning is done properly, on the release the body will act as a spring uncoiling, adding energy and power to the arms and legs. This is important on longer snaps when the ball must travel farther in as little time as possible. The snapper starts off by squatting so that the thighs are parallel to the ground. He makes sure his feet stay flat on the ground so that he can maintain stability and balance (figure 12.6). The base should allow the hips to sit in a pocket not much different from a full squat. The upper body leans forward so that the back is also parallel to the ground. The snapper's arms hang so that his elbows fit comfortably inside his knees (figure 12.7).

Figure 12.6 The feet stay flat on the ground.

Figure 12.7 The snapper's arms hang comfortably inside his knees.

The snapper's position is slightly different on a short snap. The wider base does not allow as much knee flexion. However, the principles for the upper body remain the same. The position allows the body to act as a spring about to unload, maximizing the speed at which the ball is released.

Extension

Loading the body like a spring not only increases the speed at which the snap occurs but also places the snapper's body in a position to eliminate any false moves or hitches in the motion. Everything moves at once with all the force and energy working toward the target in the shortest amount of time possible.

Eliminating any false move or hitch keeps the snapper from giving the rush team an idea of when he is going to snap the ball. This maximizes the time he has to execute the kick. In this technique, the snapper first loads the hips (figures 12.6 and 12.7), then extends not only the upper body but also the arms (figure 12.8). The snapper tries to force the ball out away from the body as far as possible while keeping the feet flat on the ground for balance and his weight back on his hips. This loads the body, allowing everything to move at once toward the target and reducing the occurrence of false moves and hitches in the snap.

Figure 12.8 Snapper extends the upper body and the arms.

Another important technique is straightening the arms as much as possible while placing the ball on its front point at a 45-degree angle (figure 12.9). This helps the snapper pull the ball on the snap and again keep everything moving toward the target while minimizing wasted motion or hitches. The snapper is trying to place himself in the most efficient position possible while allowing for consistency in the snap's speed and accuracy.

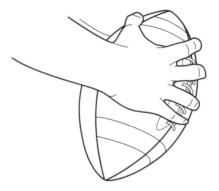

Figure 12.9 Snapper places the ball on its front end at a 45-degree angle.

Snap

Now that the snapper is in the best position possible, it's time to execute the snap itself. This part of the process requires the most work since it involves putting together all the pieces of the puzzle.

Nothing is better than good old-fashioned repetition to teach the snapper how to time the movements and the release. Once the snapper has the timing down, he is on his way to becoming a good snapper. The process begins with the snapper pulling the ball. As the ball begins to travel toward the target, the snapper's hips release, engaging the uncoiling effect. The snapper pushes his hips back by using his legs from the balls of the feet on up. This adds velocity to the snap. The snapper should transition between movements as quickly as possible, focusing on creating one smooth, flowing motion.

As the ball comes through the legs, the drive from the lower body should force the knees and hips to lock out (figure 12.10a). The idea is for the entire body to release the ball so that when the ball leaves the fingertips, the legs are straight and the hips are high, just reaching the uncoiled position (figure 12.10b). The snapper should be able to generate enough force on a punt or long snap so that his feet actually slide back, separating him from the rush and giving him time to get involved in the punt protection. As mentioned, the timing requires the most work. Starting everything in time and finishing with everything releasing together will take lots of reps.

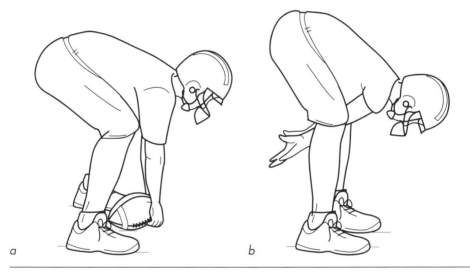

Figure 12.10 *(a)* As the ball comes through the legs, the hips and legs begin to straighten and lock out. *(b)* As the ball is released, the hips are high and the legs are straight.

Many of you are probably wondering why I haven't mentioned the head and eyes. The reason for this is that the target varies greatly depending on the confidence and experience of the snapper and his protection responsibilities. For punts the best target is the thigh of the punter's kicking leg. This spot gives the punter the easiest access to the drop point, although anywhere between the knees and the chin is an acceptable target. The best target for an extra point or field goal is the elbow of the holder's down arm. This spot allows the holder to place the ball with minimal movement. However, any target in front of the holder from the holder's chin to 6 inches off the ground is acceptable.

My best snappers rarely look at the target. They might take a quick peek before finishing the setup or while in ready position, but then they lift their heads to keep their backs flat and their hips loaded. This also allows them to see the rush and join the protection scheme. The young, inexperienced snapper, however, is best served by eyeing his target throughout the snap and then reacting to his other responsibilities. Keep this in mind when fitting a young snapper with shoulder pads and a face mask so that his movement is restricted as little as possible.

Each snapper is different and has a different rhythm, much like basketball players shooting free throws. The best snappers allow the process to work for them, but only after performing thousands of repetitions by snapping five to six days a week, 48 to 50 weeks a year. Snappers become comfortable with the snap after they've warmed up and received feedback on the placement of each snap.

Whether a snapper looks at his target or not, the process of the short snap is similar to that of the long snap. The difference is in the leg force. Because of the wider base of the short snap, the legs are straighter and the hips are higher, restricting movement. This is not a bad thing as far as the execution of the snap goes. The snapper can snap the ball with the same motion and velocity even though it's a much shorter snap because the legs, which aren't restricted, generate the majority of the velocity. The upper body and the arms and hands provide the accuracy. The snapper should not fear a fast short snap as long as he has a steady and consistent holder.

Follow-Through

The idea of the follow-through is to finish with everything going toward the target. One of most common mistakes is pulling off the ball. Snappers who are asked to help in the protection scheme are especially prone to this mistake. Pulling off the ball occurs when the snapper shortchanges the follow-through of the arms in order to get his hands up to block the oncoming rusher. This creates inconsistency in the speed and accuracy of the snap. Make sure the snapper is following through first and then reacting to any protection assignment.

The most critical part of the follow-through is the arms and hands. The arms should finish fully extended through the legs, pointing at the target (figure 12.11). This maximizes velocity on the snap as well as accuracy. Both hands should release the ball at the exact same moment, finishing in a flared position with the palms rotated so they are facing out (figure 12.12). This creates tightness of the spiral and increases accuracy. Inexperienced snappers who look at their target should be able to see the target as well as the flight of the ball between their hands. This is the part of the snap that players cheat on the most. When working with long snappers of all levels, it's imperative to emphasize the follow-through.

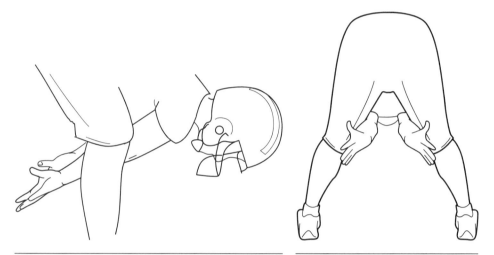

Figure 12.11 Arms finish extended through the legs, pointing at the target.

Figure 12.12 Hands finish flared with palms rotated out.

Adjustments

As with any other skill, players need to fine-tune their snapping technique once in awhile. People are not machines that are capable of repeating a task to perfection time and time again. People can get tired or sick or worn down from day-to-day pressures. Our brains and bodies don't act and react the same way every day. Sometimes rest can put us back in tune, but that's not always possible.

Sometimes the snapper needs to make adjustments based on the kind of day he is having and how it's affecting his timing. When making an adjustment, the main thing to remember is to keep it simple and understand that only a subtle change is necessary. Also, the warm-up is critical. No matter what kind of day the snapper is having, a proper warm-up is necessary. Once the snapper has warmed up, he should do 6 to 10 full-speed snaps before he even considers making any changes.

There are only two adjustments a snapper should ever have to make once he understands and can execute the basic fundamentals. The first type of adjustment is the easiest. If the ball is going left or right instead of flying straight through, the snapper is releasing the ball from one hand slightly before the other. The same is true when the spiral loses its tight rotation. If these problems persist, make sure both hands release the ball at the same time. Sometimes it may even be necessary to return to the two-hand overhead pass to work it out. The key is not to panic, but to understand what is causing the problem so it can be fixed. Normally this problem will appear during the warm-up.

The second problem that may arise is when the ball is flying high or traveling low. This adjustment is not quite as simple because it requires a delicate touch. If the ball is consistently going high or low once the snapper has completely warmed up, the guide hand needs to be moved. This is a tricky adjustment because even small movements make a world of difference. The closer the guide hand is to the back point or the higher it is on the ball, the higher the ball will sail (figure 12.13a). If the ball is sailing high, move the guide hand down slightly, remembering that small movements make a big difference. The closer the guide hand is to the front point or the lower it is on the ball, the lower the ball will travel (figure 12.13b). If the ball is traveling low, move the guide hand up, again remembering that small movements make a big difference.

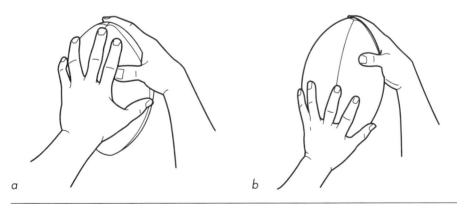

a   b

Figure 12.13 *(a)* When the guide hand is high on the ball, the ball will sail higher. *(b)* When the guide hand is low on the ball, the ball will sail lower.

The snapper must be careful moving the guide hand. He should keep it near the middle of the ball until he is certain he needs to make this adjustment. One snap is never enough to make this decision, especially early in the process. If the snapper does need to move the guide hand, he should move it up or down in small amounts; fractions of an inch usually do the trick.

Drills

We already covered many of our drills in the sections discussing the different phases, but let's review them and go over some other drills that might help. Upper-body flexibility is critical, so be sure to include some shoulder and upper-back stretches before and after workouts.

One of the first drills we discussed was playing catch. This seems like a trivial activity at times, but it helps fine-tune the release of the ball off the index finger and it helps warm up the throwing arm. You can use a weighted ball for this drill, but use it sparingly. It's the speed of the arm and not the strength that's important.

Next we touched on the two-hand overhead throw. This is a good drill for working the actual release. Overhead medicine-ball throws or pull-overs in the weight room also strengthen the shoulder girdle, but again do not allow these exercises to replace the actual throw.

Another drill we use is called snap on air. In this drill, the snapper executes the snap without using a ball so he can concentrate on body mechanics while also warming up. Again, flexibility is key, but this time in the lower body, especially the lower back, hips, hamstrings, and Achilles tendon. Any plyometric exercises to improve lower-body explosion also help generate more speed through the ball.

As part of the warm-up, the snapper snaps the ball three to five times at 10 yards. This allows him to slowly work into full-speed snaps while focusing on the timing of the start and finish. He then backs up 2 yards after 3 to 5 snaps, continuing back until he reaches normal depth.

Sometimes we play a target game after the warm-up. The target game involves choosing different parts of the body as targets. The snapper uses his snapping motion to get the ball to the target. The idea is for the snapper to make minor adjustments in order to hit the changing target. This helps the snapper learn the subtleness of the adjustments. Use this drill only with advanced snappers.

After this drill, we work on the snap and set that the snapper uses when helping in the protection scheme. First we do this drill on air and then we add a rusher who moves on the snap, forcing the snapper to snap, set, and block with the proper technique. After working on the long snap, snappers move to the short snap. Snappers take 10 to 12 snaps, using the wider base required for extra points and field goals.

Long snapping is a lot like playing golf. Knowing how to swing a club is not enough to make you a good golfer—it's all in the timing. Even the best of the best have to work at it. The key to becoming an effective long snapper is to simply snap.

CHAPTER 13

© Bill Baptist/Rice University

HOLDING FOR KICKS

STEVE KIDD

Rice University

Kicking is about confidence. To have a chance at making the kick, the kicker must have confidence in the snap, the protection, and most importantly, the holder. The holder must be athletic with soft hands and he must be confident in his ability to put the ball on the tee. He must also be able to operate in a thankless environment. The only time a holder receives recognition is when something goes wrong.

Punters, quarterbacks, and wide receivers are good candidates for holders. One walk-on receiver and one walk-on punter have earned scholarships here at Rice University by holding for us. Our scholarship punters have held the job most recently. All were confident, athletic, and could throw the ball. Obviously you need an arm if you want to run fakes, though quarterbacks are not necessarily the best candidates. I have tried to teach players who want no part of the job and it is frustrating for everyone involved, so you should select someone who wants to do it.

Huddle and Cadence

Once the decision to kick the extra point or field goal has been made, the kicker and holder head to the kicking spot while the snapper assembles the huddle on the near hash mark or numbers. If the ball is on our near hash mark, we use the numbers.

The kicker selects the placement spot, and the holder assumes his stance at the spot. (We'll discuss the stance in more detail later in the chapter.) While waiting for the huddle to break, the holder and kicker engage in a little light banter. This helps the kicker loosen up. Our holders and kickers use movie lines. One comes from the movie *A Few Good Men*. The holder says, "You want me on that wall," and the kicker responds, "You need me on that wall." Another favorite is from *Jerry McGuire*. The holder says, "Show me . . . ," and the kicker says, ". . . the money."

In the huddle, the snapper calls field goal on the long or short snap. We do not want the field goal block team to draw a bead on the snap. The snapper also is responsible for making sure that nine men are in the huddle.

After the huddle breaks, the front nine head to their position. Once in place, the snapper signals to the holder and kicker whether the snap is on the long or short count. The kicker takes his steps. The holder makes sure the kicker is ready by making eye contact until the kicker nods. Once the kicker is ready, the holder gives the snapper a hand target and calls out the cadence. The holder must be sure that the front nine are set and ready before calling the cadence. If the call is field goal on the short snap, the ball is snapped immediately after the cadence. If the call is field goal on the long snap, the snapper delays two to three counts after the cadence. You need two different cadences, one for kicking the ball and one for any fakes in the game plan.

Presnap to Kick

For the discussion on setting up from presnap to the kick, we will assume a right-footed kicker is kicking. For a left-footed kicker, simply reverse all positions.

The holder takes his position to the right of the spot or tee. He drops down on his right knee with his left knee up toward the kicker. Make sure the left foot is tucked and not in a position to interfere with ball placement. This stance makes it easier to stop a low snap, much like a catcher in baseball. Also, in this stance the holder does not expose his knee to the blocking team.

After the kicker uses his foot to mark the spot, the holder places his left pointer finger on the spot or tee and places his left elbow on the inside of his left knee. The elbow on the knee is important. When the snap is handled and the holder brings the ball to the spot, he will know he is at the spot when his elbow contacts his knee. This position is even more important when a tee is not allowed. It allows the holder to easily find the spot again. The spot should be on the inside heel of the left foot approximately 12 inches from the foot.

The holder then checks with the kicker to be sure the kicker is ready. Once the kicker is ready, the holder uses his right hand to give the snapper a target (figure 13.1). To give a target, the holder's hand must be open and just slightly below shoulder level. He gives the cadence and awaits the snap.

Figure 13.1 The holder has marked the spot and given a target.

As the ball is delivered, both hands reach for the ball with thumbs together (figure 13.2). The holder concentrates on the tip of the ball. If the snap is low, the holder uses his left hand to stop the ball and his right hand to trap the top of it.

Figure 13.2 Catching the snap.

After catching the snap, the holder brings the ball to the spot or tee. The holder's left hand shifts to the top of the ball while his right hand grips the front of the ball. When the left elbow hits the left knee, the ball is placed on the spot or tee.

For a laces-back snap, the right hand rotates the seams. The left hand actually holds the ball. I teach the holder to use his first three fingers (index, middle, and ring) to hold the ball (figure 13.3). The holder should never spin the ball if the laces are back. If the laces are back, the holder simply uses his right hand to rotate the laces out of sight, removing his hand as quickly as possible.

Most kickers like the ball to be slightly slanted away from them. To accomplish this slant, the holder pulls the ball a couple of degrees toward himself. He must not apply too much pressure to the top of the ball; too much pressure makes the ball feel heavy to the kicker at impact. The holder should use just enough pressure to keep the ball on the spot or tee.

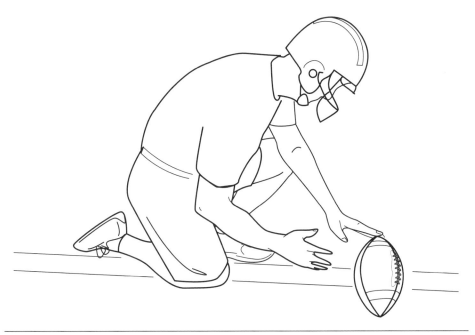

Figure 13.3 Holder holds the ball on the spot or tee with the first three fingers of the left hand.

A great deep snapper can minimize the need to spin the laces. In four years as our deep snapper, Ryan Pontbriand, who was drafted in the fifth round of the NFL draft in 2003, never had a laces-back snap. However, not everybody can be that lucky.

The snapper and holder need to do tons of repetitions to become familiar with each other. If the laces are consistently back on short snaps, have the snapper start his snap with a passing grip on the laces. If the laces are still back, have him slightly rotate the ball in his right hand (right-handed snapper) off the laces toward the right side of the ball. The speed on his snaps must be consistent. On the short snap, it is not critical for the snapper to have his hands on the laces. Through trial and error the snapper will find the grip that best matches his snapping speed and laces-back snaps should become nonexistent.

Things do go haywire every so often. If the laces are dead back, tell the holder to use his right hand to rotate the laces out of sight. He must never spin the ball. The laces do not need to be completely forward; they just need to be out of the kicker's view. I like for the holder to use the right hand to rotate the ball because that way the kicker never sees anything but the ball. If the laces are dead back or toward the kicker, the holder uses a clockwise rotation, pulling the ball toward the front. If the laces are toward the holder, the holder pushes the ball counterclockwise toward the front. In either case, the left hand holds the ball while the right hand adjusts it.

Bad-Snap Procedures

If a major malfunction occurs and the ball cannot be placed on the spot or tee, the holder yells, "Fire, fire, fire." An extra point or field goal is kicked in 1.2 to 1.3 seconds, which does not give the holder a lot of time to decide if he can rescue a bad snap. It is more important to get the snap down than to abandon it and rely on the fire call. The holder must rely on his instincts to make a sound judgment call.

"Fire, fire, fire" tells the tight ends and wings to run predetermined routes. The tight ends run 10- to 25-yard flag routes depending on the situation (figure 13.4). The shorter route works on an extra point. The wings run an arrow route at the first-down marker or just inside the goal line on an extra point.

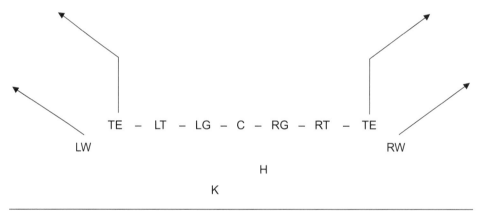

Figure 13.4 On a bad snap, the tight ends run flag routes and the wings run arrow routes.

The holder can roll out to either side depending on how the ball bounces. The holder must be able to handle pressure and make good decisions. If no one is open, the holder must either try to run the ball in or throw it away. Obviously we do not want an errant or ill-advised pass to be intercepted and returned for a score, so the holder must be able to make quick, sound decisions.

Snap-and-Hold Practice

Let me state the obvious: Performance improves through repetition. The snapper and holder need reps every day to ensure consistency and success. The snap and hold might be the single most important part of the game that is taken for granted.

Do not let your snapper and holder lapse into complacency. I have our snapper and holder execute 10 perfect snaps and holds at the end of each practice. This is in addition to our regular practice routine. If one exchange is not perfect, they run three gassers. Everything must be perfect, including the laces facing forward. These snaps help our snapper and holder remain focused, and it reinforces the importance of the snaps.

We also practice responding to bad snaps. The snapper should not be involved in this session. The coach throws snaps at the holder (high, low, inside, outside). It never hurts to prepare for a possible disaster.

Our current snapper and holder even snap in the hallway of our hotel the night before and the day of our games. They were never instructed to do this; they simply take a lot of pride in their operation, which benefits us tremendously. Stress the importance of the snap to your snapper and holder, and in time they might begin practicing in the hallways, too, leading your team to a better chance for success.

CHAPTER 14

© DePauw University

RETURNING PUNTS AND KICKOFFS

BILL LYNCH
DePauw University

No single factor affects the strategy of a football game like field position, and nothing affects field position like the kicking game. Teams that expect to win must excel in all phases of special teams play. Most of us work hard at punt protection because we know how dramatically a poor snap or blocked punt can affect the outcome of a game. Likewise, a mishandled punt or kickoff can result in a turnover or a tremendous loss of field position, a mistake that could be the deciding factor in an important game.

The physical characteristics of a successful returner may vary, but he must be fundamentally sound and use great judgment at all times. The punt or kickoff returner plays on an island, and he must be prepared to perform under pressure. We all have seen a return that turned the tide of a big game, but we must remember that the return began with solid execution of the fundamentals.

In this chapter I outline the fundamentals for punt and kickoff returners. I include drills that can help a returner develop the confidence and skills to execute in the tough game conditions that occur during a football season.

Fundamentals for Punt Returners

The returner's alignment must allow him to field the ball. On average, 15 yards are lost when the ball hits the ground. The punt returner should align 40 yards from the line of scrimmage (figure 14.1). This general rule is for returning a punt from an average punter when there are no significant wind conditions.

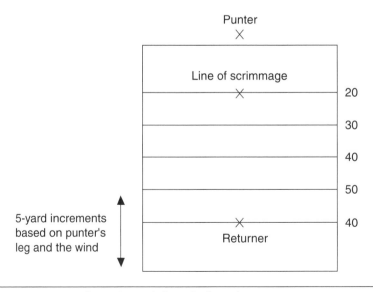

Figure 14.1 Returner aligns 40 yards from the line of scrimmage.

The returner may need to adjust his alignment to the punter and the wind conditions. The returner should align himself according to the punter's season average, adjusting for a very good or poor punter. If wind conditions will affect the distance the ball is kicked, the returner should adjust his alignment in 5-yard increments. For example, if the punter is kicking with a fairly strong wind, the returner might align 45 yards from the line of scrimmage. If the punter is punting with a stiff wind, the returner might align 50 yards from the line of scrimmage. If the punter is kicking into a stiff wind, the returner should move up toward the line of scrimmage in 5-yard increments. The pregame warm-ups should give the returner a feel for the wind and how it will affect the ball.

If the ball is being punted inside 40 yards or inside the punter's range, the returner should align with his heels on the 10-yard line. The returner should never back up from that alignment to field a ball inside the 10-yard line (figure 14.2). If the returner is aligned on the 20-yard line, he should have a sense of how many retreat steps it would take to get back to the 10-yard line. Once he feels he is at the 10, he should not back up farther to field a punt.

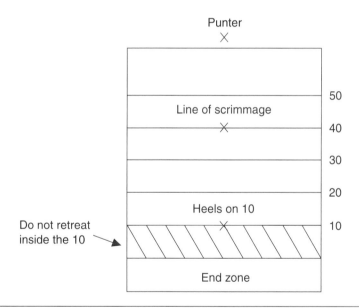

Figure 14.2 The returner lines up on the 10-yard line if the ball is being punted inside 40 yards or inside the punter's range.

Before each punt, the returner must be aware of the score, time, field position, game conditions, and the return or block that has been called. The returner should always be able to see the punter's foot so he can see the ball. If necessary, the returner should move a little to the left or the right to see the ball as it is kicked.

Catching Punts

The most important part of each punt return is catching the ball. The returner must sprint to get into position to catch any balls he can. As mentioned, the return team loses an average of 15 yards each time the ball hits the ground. The returner needs to work to get squared up when catching the ball (figure 14.3). He does not want to be turned toward the sideline when fielding the ball.

Figure 14.3 The returner's shoulders are square to the line of scrimmage when he catches the ball.

If the ball is kicked to the left or right, the returner should sprint to that side and get in position to catch the ball square to the line of scrimmage. He should not face the sideline. If the ball is kicked deep over his head, he should open his hips and run to get behind and underneath the ball. He should not backpedal to get behind the ball; he must turn and run.

The returner needs to get underneath the ball. He must watch the ball's flight pattern in order to judge where the ball will come down. If the returner understands the flight pattern (figure 14.4), he will have a better opportunity to get squared up and underneath the ball. Here is a list of where the ball will come down in different flight patterns.

- Nose up: The ball will fall short or come straight down from its highest point (figure 14.4a)
- Nose over: The ball will drive deep (figure 14.4b)
- Nose right: The ball will fall to the right (figure 14.4c)
- Nose left: The ball will fall to the left (figure 14.4d)
- Knuckle ball: The ball will fall straight down from its highest point (figure 14.4e)

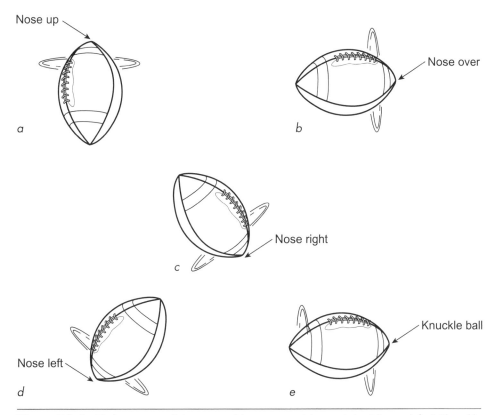

Figure 14.4   Flight patterns: *(a)* nose up; *(b)* nose over; *(c)* nose right; *(d)* nose left; *(e)* knuckle ball.

Once underneath the ball, the returner should try to get into a rocker-step position. This position allows the returner to see the field and accelerate upfield after making the catch. In the rocker step, the returner starts in a football position with a staggered stance. He adjusts his weight from the front leg to the back leg with a slight rocking motion. For the returner, the key to success is to catch the ball with his momentum moving forward. Once underneath the ball, an advanced returner may take a peek at the gunners and coverage men to see where they are before returning his eyes to the football. A less experienced returner should keep his eyes on the ball at all times.

The best way to catch the ball is in a cradle position. The returner should fine-tune his feet, getting the feet underneath the body so that the ball drops into the pocket—the area between the arms and the body—the same way every time. He should get his hands out where he can see them. He should keep his elbows in, providing a backstop for the ball. The forearms should never be the only stopping surface.

As he catches the ball, the returner should give slightly with the ball. He should look the ball all the way into his hands and into the tuck position, and then accelerate upfield. If the returner ever drops the ball, he must get on the ball immediately.

Calling for the Fair Catch

For a fair catch, the returner should get underneath the ball before giving a nice high signal for the fair catch. Once the returner gives the fair-catch signal, he should focus on the ball, knowing that he is totally protected.

On a ball kicked low and short, the returner must sprint to get to the ball and may make a fair-catch signal on his way. If the ball has a lot of hang time, he should give a "Peter" call so that the antigunners (corners) get out of the way.

Fielding a Bouncing Punt

If the returner is unable to get to a punted ball, he should allow the ball one good bounce before fielding it, as long as it is safe. The returner should place himself 10 yards behind the ball and be square to the line of scrimmage. Giving the ball 10 yards allows the returner to field a good bounce and avoid a bad one. The returner does not want the bouncing ball to hit him. He should never play the second bounce.

The returner must know what type of surface he is playing on and what kind of bounce he will see. The ball bounces higher and harder on an artificial surface. A grass surface causes the ball to bounce softer and lower.

If the returner is unable to catch the ball, he should wave his arms and yell "Peter" repeatedly until the punt return team hears him and gets away from the ball. It is the returner's responsibility to make sure the ball does not bounce and hit him or any member of the return team.

Using the 10-Yard Rule

If the returner is backed up and using the 10-yard rule, he should never retreat to field a ball. He should put his heels on the 10-yard line and not move backward.

If the ball is going to land behind the 10-yard line, the returner should use a draw technique (figure 14.5). In a draw technique, the returner draws the coverage to himself, away from the ball. The returner does not use a fair-catch signal, but rather simulates the catch. He must be a good actor to sell the fake catch to the coverage team.

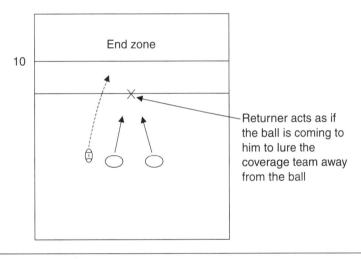

Figure 14.5 Draw technique.

If the ball is not going to drop inside the 10-yard line, the returner should make every effort to catch the ball. If it is a punt-safe situation, the returner may want to make a fair catch.

One of the most common mistakes returners make is aligning on the 20-yard line and retreating behind the 10-yard line to field the ball. The returner must know where he is on the field and practice retreating from the 20-yard line to get the steps down.

Remember, any ball touched by the opponent but not blown dead can be advanced at no risk, and all muffed punts must be recovered.

Punt Catching Drills

Punt returners have many choices when it comes to choosing drills. They can use drills both with a punter and without a punter to improve technique and fielding success.

Drills With a Punter   The best punt catching drill is catching punts directly from the punter. It is important for the returner to practice catching all different types of punts off the punter's foot (with the wind, against the wind, deep balls, short balls, knuckle balls, and so on).

The next phase of the drill is incorporating gunners and antigunners. Align gunners and antigunners 15 yards away from the returner. After the ball is kicked, the coach releases the gunners toward the returner. The gunners break down around the returner. The returner fields the punt as if it were a game situation. If he would fair catch that particular punt in a game, then he should do so in the drill. If he would return the punt, he should field the ball and accelerate upfield, making a move on the gunner if necessary (figure 14.6). The point of this drill is to simulate what the returner will see and feel in the game.

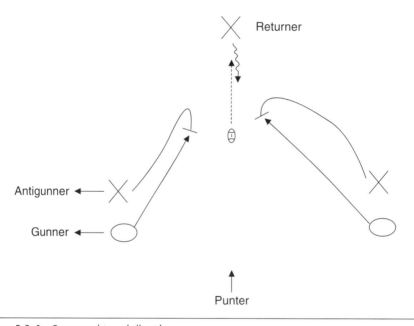

Figure 14.6   Punt catching drill with gunners.

Another good drill is the two-ball drill. In this drill, the returner holds on to a football while he waits for the punter to punt the ball. When the ball is punted, the returner aligns himself underneath the ball to make the catch. The returner tosses up the ball that he is holding, catches the punted ball, and then catches the ball he tossed. The returner's goal is to catch both balls without either one hitting the ground.

For the back to the ball drill, the returner faces away from where the punter is kicking and waits for the ball to be kicked. Once the ball is kicked, a coach or another player yells, "Go," and the returner spins around, finds the ball, and makes the catch.

For the up–down drill, the returner faces the punter and waits for the ball to be kicked. Once the punter kicks the ball, the returner does an up–down and then tries to get underneath the ball and make the catch. (For the up–down, the returner hits the ground with his chest then bounces back up as quickly as possible.)

The 10-yard line drill simulates the situation where the returner uses the 10-yard rule. In this drill, the returner practices the draw technique, faking the catch to entice the gunners. He can also practice making the catch if the ball is not going to fall inside the 10-yard line. The returner lines up on the 20-yard line to get a feel for how many retreat steps he must take to get to the 10-yard line. He can first walk these steps without a ball. The punter punts the ball and the returner fields it. Any type of punt will do.

Drills Without a Punter   The one-hop drill lets the returner give a poorly kicked ball one good bounce before returning it. In this drill, a coach stands 15 yards away from the returner and throws the ball into the turf. The ball naturally will bounce in different ways. The returner must decide when to field a good bounce and when to get away from a bad bounce.

In the deep kick drill, the returner must field a ball kicked deep past him. The coach stands 15 yards from the returner and throws the ball behind the returner, simulating a deep kick. The returner must work on opening his hips and getting back behind the ball to field it.

The short kick drill focuses on fielding a punt that is kicked short of the returner. It gives the returner practice sprinting upfield to field a short kick. The returner can practice signaling for a fair catch as he comes up to field the ball. The coach stands about 15 yards from the returner and throws a ball up in the air, short of the returner. This forces the returner to come up quickly to make the play.

The sideline kick drill gives the returner practice returning punts kicked to the right or left. This drill is the same as the deep and short kick drills except the coach throws the ball to the returner's right or left.

In the beginning, have the returner practice the drills without a punter. After the returner has done each drill, you can combine them into one and have the returner adjust to all of the different kicks.

When coaching punt returners during practice, remember that the returner must accelerate up the field for at least 5 to 10 yards after the catch. Returners have to practice good habits so that the habits will carry over to the game.

Fundamentals for Kickoff Returners

The kickoff returner should align at the 5-yard line, 3 yards outside the hash marks (figure 14.7). This is for a two-deep return team. The returner needs to know the opposing team's kicker, his average distance, and where he likes to place the ball. He also needs to know what type of kick the kicker likes and what kind of hang time he gets. A scouting report should help the returner know where to align based on the kicker's tendencies.

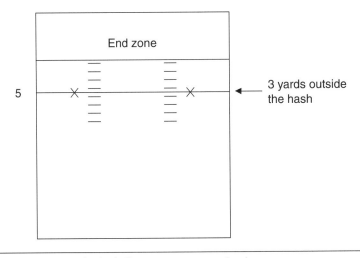

Figure 14.7 Alignment for kickoff returners in a two-back setup.

The returner must also be aware of the wind and if it is at the kicker's back or against him, if it's a crosswind, or if there is no wind. All of these factors will alter where the returner should align.

A returner must know the rules on the kickoff return. All kicks are live and if the ball is on the ground or bounces, he needs to get on it. A returner can call for a fair catch on a bloop kick and be protected. A ball touched by the return team or muffed by the returner that goes into the end zone may be downed. You must constantly review these situations with the kickoff returners.

In a two-deep setup, communication between the two returners is crucial. One of the returners should be in charge of balls kicked between the two of them. The returner in charge should use a "Me, me, me" or "You, you, you" call. The off returner should always secure the kick—make sure the ball is fielded cleanly—before he carries out his blocking assignment. On a squib kick, the off returner should back up his partner, being sure to give him 10 yards to allow for a big bounce. When a ball is kicked into the end zone, the off returner should help his buddy decide whether or not to return the ball.

As a general rule, returners should down a ball kicked 3 yards deep or more and return a ball kicked less than 3 yards deep, depending on the height and hang time of the kick. The keys are communication and no hesitation.

As he lines up, the returner should always know where a return is designed to go. He also should be aware of the situation, score, time, and field conditions. He should look for the kicker's angle to anticipate a directional kick. Again, scouting reports will help reveal the kicker's tendencies.

Catching Kickoffs

The number one rule when catching kickoffs is to field all kicks. Remember, kick returners must know the rules. Because the ball is live and can bounce in different ways, the kickoff returner must field the kick in the air if at all possible.

Catching the ball first is the key to any good return. The returner needs to look the ball into his hands and all the way into the pocket, the area between his arm and body. It helps if the returner tries to overemphasize looking the ball all the way in the pocket. The returner should cover the point of the ball as he tucks it away. Once the ball is tucked away, the returner should let the ball swing in a natural rhythm as he runs. He must have great ball security. When the returner anticipates getting hit, he should cover the ball with both hands. Even if the returner breaks into the open field, he cannot relax. Many fumbles occur when a defender pursuing from behind strips the ball.

The kickoff returner must work to get square and underneath the ball. This allows him to get into a rocker-step position so that he can accelerate up the field following the catch. It is especially important for the returner to sprint to get square and underneath the ball in the case of wedge return teams because most wedge teams set their wedge on the returner's alignment.

If a ball is kicked to the corner, the kickoff returner should sprint to get square and underneath the ball. He needs to get in a rocker-step position on these kicks as well. He must get to the ball first and then make a decision on fielding the ball.

The returner should not field a ball that is going sideways toward the sideline, especially if the returner feels like his momentum will take him out of bounds. If the ball looks like it will go out of bounds, the return team has a chance to get the ball in a decent field position. The ball also could bounce into the end zone.

The returner needs to field squib kicks cleanly and safely. He must be sure to get square to the ball, field it, and then move directly up the field.

The returner should think "score" every time. He wants to locate a seam and then accelerate. The kick returner should avoid dancing around. He needs to find the seam and get vertical up the field with great speed.

Again, a general rule for touchbacks is if the ball is 3 or more yards deep in the end zone, the returner should down the ball. If it is less than 3 yards deep, the returner should return the kick, depending on the hang time of the kick.

Kickoff Catching Drills

Kickoff returners can use the following drills to improve their catching technique. Drills both with and without a kicker are featured.

Drills With a Kicker   The best return catching drill is catching kickoffs directly from the kicker's foot. The returner needs to get used to catching all kinds of kicks, so the kicker should give the returner the chance to catch deep kicks, short kicks, kicks in the corners, and bloop kicks.

The returner also needs to practice catching kicks in all wind conditions (wind with the kicker, wind against the kicker, and crosswind kicks). This helps the returner get a feel for what the ball will do in different wind conditions.

Drills with a kicker provide gamelike situations so that the return man can practice what he will see in a game.

Drills Without a Kicker   In the communication drill, two returners align as if receiving a kickoff. The coach throws a ball between the returners to simulate a kickoff coming between them (figure 14.8). (You can also use a Jugs machine to simulate the kickoff.) The returner in charge decides who should field the ball and makes the "Me, me, me" or "You, you, you" call. This drill improves communication between the two returners.

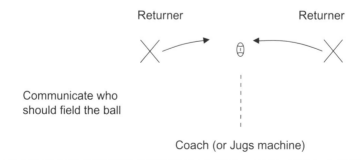

Figure 14.8 Communication drill.

In the squib kick drill, the coach stands 10 to 15 yards in front of the returner. The coach throws the ball into the ground, simulating a squib kick. The returner stays square and in front of the ball while fielding the kick. Once he fields the kick, he tucks it away and goes straight up the field.

The angle kick drill helps the returner practice getting square and in a good rocker-step position underneath a ball that is kicked into a corner. He lines up as usual and the coach simulates the kickoff to the corner (figure 14.9). (You can also use a Jugs machine to simulate the kick.) The returner sprints over to the ball, gets square to the ball, makes the catch, and accelerates up the field.

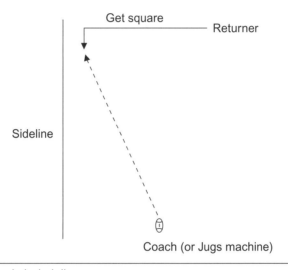

Figure 14.9 Angle kick drill.

In all drills, the returner should accelerate up the field at least 10 yards after catching each kickoff. This reinforces the habit of catching the ball and getting up the field with great speed.

You must cover a number of situations with returners. The coach's attention to detail when covering these situations will give the team the best chance to avoid critical errors when fielding punts or kickoffs. Having solid fundamentals and performing drills to reinforce these skills are the keys to a successful return game.

CHAPTER 15

© Human Kinetics

DEVELOPING SPECIAL TEAMS PLAYERS

JOE DEFOREST
Oklahoma State University

The philosophy of special teams at Oklahoma State is that nothing is more important than the kicking game. One out of five plays in a game is some form of kicking play. The difference between winning and losing is usually found in this area.

What special teams do for a team is dictate field position. Every time a football is kicked, teams exchange huge chunks of field position. The better you cover, the worse your opponent's field position will be. The better you block and return, the better your field position will be. That is the obvious benefit of skilled special teams.

Big plays usually happen when a team or player is unprepared for a situation. When a team is prepared, it has the chance to capitalize on the break. The ability to take advantage of breaks in the kicking game marks the difference between winning and losing many games. When a team neglects the attention required to develop a proper kicking game, they become victims of these bad breaks. You can only have a successful kicking game if you consider it to be the equal of the other two parts of the game, offense and defense.

Special teams have other benefits as well. They unify a ball club, bringing together players who have diverse objectives and pointing them in the same direction. In special teams there are no 12-play drives: You get one shot. That boosts team spirit because offensive and defensive players come together for a specific down. A cornerback is a cornerback and a fullback is a fullback, but you might have a cornerback and fullback side by side on the punting team. Special teams bring offense and defense together and give them a singleness of purpose, which ultimately is to win!

It takes a special individual to be on special teams. Such a person has the following characteristics:

- *Attitude.* An individual's attitude will surface on special teams. Only players with outstanding attitudes are selected. Playing on a special team is, of course, extra work, so players must want to be part of the kicking game. Make it a point to praise players for a job well done. Success will bring great attitudes to players on special teams.

- *Work habits.* An individual may be an outstanding athlete, but he cannot be on special teams if he doesn't develop good work habits. While their teammates are taking showers and talking to reporters, these players hone their unique talents as members of the special teams. An individual who is not willing to work and make a sacrifice cannot be part of the special teams unit.

- *Toughness.* Some of the best hits occur during special teams play; consequently only the tough can perform here. Toughness isn't just physical. Players must also possess mental toughness. A successful player is confident and comfortable in his role regardless of game pressure or how tired he is.

- *Intelligence.* There is so much to learn in such a short period of time that only intelligent football players can be part of the special teams. An individual who doesn't learn quickly cannot be on special teams.

- *Talent.* This is the least important requirement for our special teams. Certainly a player has to be able to run well and do some other athletic things, but talent doesn't determine who plays on special teams. When talent is combined with the previous ingredients—attitude, work ethic, toughness, and intelligence—you get pride. Pride means success!

- *Unselfishness.* Unselfishness refers to the way a player feels about the overall success of the team. The unselfish player respects his teammates. He likes himself and he likes his teammates. He is confident that the team is going to be successful. When you put together a group of people with the right attitude, teamwork naturally results. On a team, individuals respect each other and are willing to work together as a unit to make sure they do not let each other down. When teamwork happens, the result is excellence. Excellence comes about when everybody carries out his job to precision with a great deal of confidence and pride. Success comes from excellence, excellence comes from teamwork, and teamwork comes from attitude.

Assigning Players to Special Teams

Picking the right personnel for the right unit is the most important thing a coach can do. The first thing you must be aware of is how many snaps a player will play on offense and defense. A player's productivity tends to decline after more than 80 total plays unless he is in extraordinary condition. Our philosophy at Oklahoma State is for starters in skill positions on offense or defense to be a part of at least two special teams units. This sends a message to the entire team about the importance of the kicking game.

Each unit has specific athletic needs. Picking the right starters is the key. The two units we will talk about are the kickoff team and the punt block and return team.

Kickoff Team

We want great tacklers on the kickoff team. For the most part, the kickoff team consists of defensive players. The safeties should be the most reliable players and should have great speed (corners). Contain players should be the smartest players. They must understand leverage and be able to make plays in space (safeties). We want the other six players on the kickoff unit to be fearless and unselfish (linebackers, fast defensive ends, and fullbacks). One of the drills we use to evaluate these players is the kickoff cover drill (figure 15.1).

The coverage player (1) runs across the field in a 10-yard lane. The first phase of coverage is the sprint zone. The blocker (2) on top of the numbers

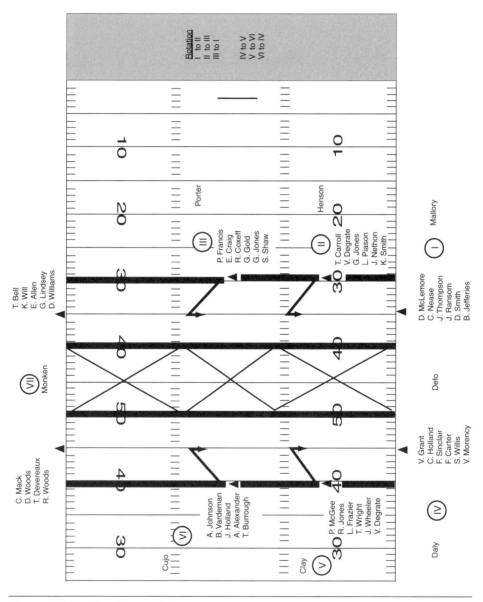

Figure 15.1 Kickoff cover drill.

gets to the hash mark and tries to block the coverage player. The coverage player now employs the second phase of coverage, the avoid zone, and works to get back in his lane. Once the coverage player clears the first blocker, the second-level blocker (3) gets to the far hash mark and tries to block the coverage player. Once the coverage player reaches the second-level blocker in the attack zone, he needs to know where the ball carrier (4) is in relation to the blocker.

We let blockers use one of three techniques, which include two-hand butt and separate and shed; long arm to the ball side; and butt and swim or rip. We never want coverage players to try to avoid a block in the attack zone. They don't have enough room to get back in their lane, and avoiding the block will create back creases in the lane distribution.

After working this drill, you will be able to evaluate players who can make a play in space. You can also film this drill for a great teaching tool. You can isolate each player on video and work through each scenario.

Punt Block and Return Team

The players in this unit must be able to block punts as well as set up for returns because using a different group for each call tells the opponent which play is coming.

When we teach an athlete how to block a punt, we start at the end of the play. First, the player sets up two feet in front of the punter and the punter takes one step and punches the football. At this point the coach can give precise instructions on hand placement. This step eliminates fear of the sting of the ball. Second, the player backs up 5 yards from the block point and walks or jogs to the spot. This helps him learn to adjust his hands and eyes if he overruns the block point. Third, the player goes full speed from 10 yards away, getting off on the snap. Coaches will be able to see if the player has a knack for blocking a kick or if he can be taught the correct way to do it.

When setting up a return, you must not only teach assignments but also how the defender will react once he recognizes where the ball is being returned. One drill we use to develop this technique is pop and trail (figure 15.2). In this drill a middle return is set up. Each player's assignment is to attack the outside shoulder of his man. As the defender starts to fan to his coverage lane, the player releases and stays inside, half a yard behind his man.

Once the defender recognizes where the return is going, he reacts accordingly. Punt return blockers must anticipate the defender's reaction and not overrun to create an undercut by the defender. As long as the blocker can keep his backside between the returner and the defender and mirror the defender's actions, the defender will be shielded from the returner.

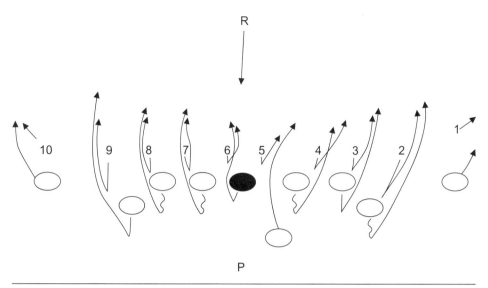

Figure 15.2 Pop and trail drill.

This drill uses the wings, tackles, guards, center, and personal protector. Two players go at the same time. You can also emphasize punt coverage in this drill. Teach the punting team how to counter a pop and trail technique.

A second drill we use in our punt return game teaches players how to set up a wall return. We do this drill in three phases: on air, scattered coverage, and full punt and cover (figure 15.3).

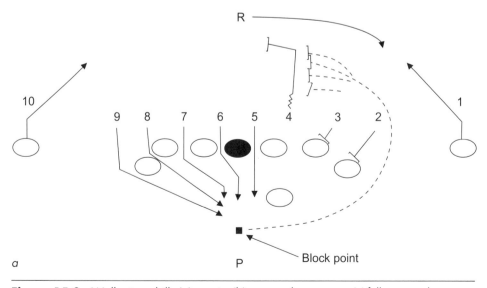

Figure 15.3 Wall return drill: *(a)* on air; *(b)* scattered coverage; *(c)* full punt and cover.

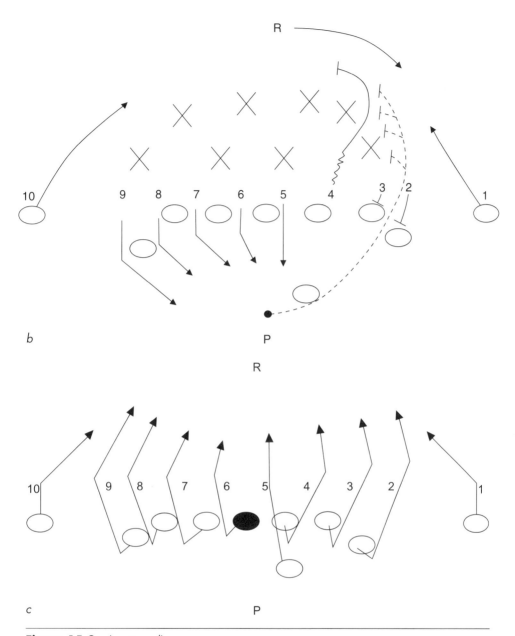

Figure 15.3 (continued)

Phase one, on air, is the first step to teaching ball getoff and wall spacing. We use cones to simulate a punting team formation. The coach moves the ball on cadence. Each player executes his block assignment and then starts to the wall. The biggest coaching point is that players who are blocked should immediately get to the wall. As the player sprints through the block point (assuming the punt is not blocked), he locates the point man in the wall (4). We try to have 5-yard spacing between each member of the wall. Once the returner catches the ball, the wall attacks toward the middle of the field. When the ball carrier passes a player, that player turns and escorts the ball carrier to the end zone. Players must never block back once the returner has gone by them.

Phase two, scattered coverage, is the same as on air except there is live coverage down the field. Each X in figure 15.3b simulates a player in his coverage lane. The drill starts the same as on air except on the coach's command the coverage team reacts to the returner. The emphasis is on not letting defenders split the wall. When the point man sets the wall, the next player in the wall cannot let any defender between him and the point man. The third player in the wall cannot let a defender between him and the second man in the wall, and so on throughout the entire wall. Once players get a feel for the spacing and are setting the wall with great effort, move on to the last phase.

Phase three, full punt and cover, is the total package. We use our number two punt team versus our number one punt return unit in a live (no tackling) drill. The emphasis here, of course, is on the speed of the game.

A third method we use to develop special teams is a circuit drill. Once we have chosen personnel, we try to perfect their techniques in a circuit drill. As figure 15.4 shows, the coach responsible for that part of the kicking unit works in a controlled setting, targeting the specifics of that position. This gets every coach involved and virtually every player working on some aspect of the kicking game. Here is what we work on in this particular circuit:

- Punt returners: Judging a punt in a red-zone situation.
- Snapper and punter: Hanging the ball inside the 10-yard line.
- Guards and holdup men: Hanging middle coverage and defending gunners in the red zone.
- Interim punt versus punt return: Working pop and trail on each side.
- Punt blockers: Taking the ball off the foot.
- Kickoff returners: Catching the kickoff and communicating with each other (two returners).
- Back wedge (fullbacks and tight ends): Setting up the timing and techniques of their kickoff return blocks.
- Kickers: Varying hang time to mix up timing for back wedge and returners.
- Frontline kickoff return: Setting with depth and positioning and technique.

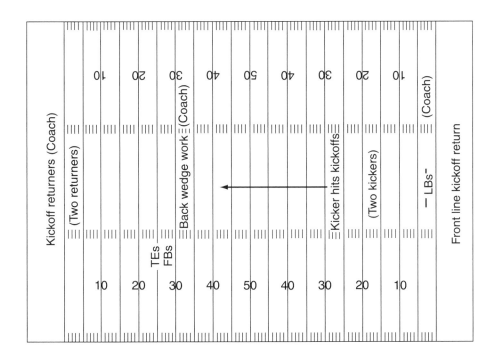

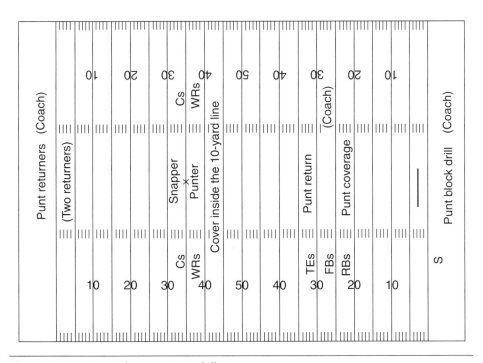

Figure 15.4 Special teams circuit drill.

Extra Point and Field Goal Unit

This unit is made up mostly of first-string offensive linemen, with the most dependable fullbacks in the wing positions and the tight ends in the tight end positions. Ideally the snapper is bigger than the punt snapper, though this might not always be possible.

Snap consistency is the number one priority of the extra point and field goal unit, so the holder is incredibly important. Although many teams use a wide receiver or quarterback as the holder, we prefer the punter to be the holder because he is used to handling snaps. Also, if the punter is the holder he will be available when the specialists are ready to practice the timing of the play.

Evaluating Special Teams Players

As with any offensive or defensive position, it is important to grade each special teams player. That takes a lot of time and effort, but if you are going to emphasize the kicking game, you must make each player accountable for his play.

The system we came up with is a simple chart for each unit (table 15.1). Every player's name at two deep for each phase is on the chart. We give a

Table 15.1 Evaluating Special Teams: Kickoff Return

| Name | Position | Kickoff | | | | | |
		1	2	3	4	%	Comments
Player 1	LT	TB	+	—	+	66	
Player 2	LG	TB	+	+	+	100	
Player 3	C	TB	—	+	+	66	
Player 4	RG	TB	+	+	—	66	
Player 5	RT	TB	+	+	—	66	
Player 6	LTE	TB	+	+	—	66	
Player 7	LFB	TB	+	+	+	100	
Player 8	RFB	TB	+	+	+	100	
Player 9	RTE	TB	+	+	—	66	
Player 10	LR	TB	+	+	+	100	
Player 11	RR	TB	+	—	+	66	

TB = touchback

plus (+) or minus (–) grade on each play and a percentage grade for each game. This is a great way to see exactly who is making plays or who is not getting the job done.

One way to evaluate the special teams unit as a whole is to look at conference and national rankings in each of the statistically kept categories. For example, we keep a running tally of where we rank in net punt yards, punt return yards, kickoff coverage, and kickoff return yards. We combine the rankings in each phase and come up with a total to show where each team ranks in our conference (table 15.2). We also do this with the national rankings at the end of the year. This system not only provides an evaluation of the kicking game, but it is also an excellent motivational tool for athletes.

Table 15.2 **Rankings for Big 12 Special Teams (2003)**

Overall national ranking	Team	Punt return	Kickoff coverage	Net punting	Kickoff return	Total
1	Oklahoma State	1	1	2	9	13
2	Oklahoma	5	3	4	5	17
3	Kansas State	6	8	3	3	20
4	Nebraska	9	10	1	1	21
5	Texas	4	1	6	11	22
6	Kansas	3	4	11	7	25
7	Missouri	2	5	12	8	27
8	Texas A&M	12	7	8	2	29
9	Texas Tech	8	6	5	10	29
10	Colorado	7	9	10	6	32
11	Baylor	10	12	7	4	33
12	Iowa State	11	10	8	12	41

Teaching Special Teams Skills

At Oklahoma State, we believe that to be successful in the kicking game we must teach each athlete his job and all the coaching points involved. This means each player needs individual instruction. Our special teams staff assignments are planned out not only to work with the coach's area of expertise, but also to make sure the entire staff has something invested in the kicking game. Here is how we break down the coaching responsibilities for special teams:

- Head coach: Oversees all phases of special teams play; makes critical gameday calls such as fakes, punts, field goal attempts, and so on.
- Wide receivers coach: Coaches the kickoff and punt returners.
- Safeties coach: Coaches the gunners on the punt and the destroyers on the punt return.
- Offensive line coach: Coaches the field goal protection unit.
- Running backs coach: Coaches half of the punt team and kickoff return team.
- Tight ends coach: Coaches half of the punt team and kickoff return team.
- Special teams coordinator: Coaches the hot spots in all phases of special teams play.

Organization and installation are also important for developing a sound kicking game and developing special teams players. When installing each phase, focus on one unit a day. This gives the athletes a chance to learn the technique, perform it, evaluate their performance on videotape, and immediately correct the technique at the next practice. It is not advantageous to move on to a different phase until each skill is perfected, one unit at a time. Following is an installation schedule we used at Oklahoma State.

Monday

Walk-through (8:30-8:40 A.M.)	Punt return: pop and trail
Practice (full) (15 minutes)	Extra point and field goal: punt return (middle)
Meetings (3:15-3:30 P.M.)	Punt coverage
Walk-through (4:25-4:35 P.M.)	Punt and cover: release drill
Practice (full) (15 minutes)	Extra point and field goal: punt and cover
Meetings (8:45-9:00 P.M.)	Kickoff coverage
Walk-through (10:10-10:20 P.M.)	Extra point and field goal: (fire, apart) red stay and red fire

Tuesday

Walk-through (8:30-8:40 A.M.)	Kickoff cover drill
Practice (full) (15 minutes)	Extra point and field goal, kickoff cover drill

Meetings (3:15-3:30 P.M.)	Kickoff return: stackers and bomb coverage
Walk-through (4:25-4:35 P.M.)	Kickoff return: twist
Practice (full) (15 minutes)	Extra point and field goal, kickoff return
Meetings (8:45-9:00 P.M.)	Kickoff return: surprise onsides, reception after safety, pooch, fair catch
Walk-through (10:10-10:20 P.M.)	Hand team versus right, left, deep

Wednesday

Meetings (8:15-8:30 A.M.)	Review kickoff return
Meetings (2:30-2:45 P.M.)	Punt block: tight, offensive formation, blocked
Walk-through (3:30-3:40 P.M.)	Punt block
Practice (full)	Mock game
Meeting (8:45-9:00 P.M.)	Review scrimmage
Walk-through (10:10-10:30 P.M.)	Correct mistakes

Thursday

Walk-through (8:30-8:40 A.M.)	Punt: fakes and stingers
Practice (full) (15 minutes)	Extra point and field goal (hurry): punt
Meeting (3:15-3:30 P.M.)	Kickoff return: trap
Walk-through (4:25-4:35 P.M.)	Kickoff return: trap
Practice (full) (15 minutes)	Extra point and field goal (hurry): kickoff return (trap)
Meeting (8:45-9:00 P.M.)	Kickoff cover and onsides
Walk-through (10:10-10:20 P.M.)	Kickoff cover and onsides: reverse, throwback, pooch, fair catch, kick after safety

Friday

Walk-through (8:30-8:40 A.M.)	Onsides kick
Practice (full) (15 minutes)	Extra point and field goal: punt
Meeting (3:15-3:30 P.M.)	Onsides kick
Walk-through (4:25-4:35 P.M.)	Punt: fake
Practice (full) (15 minutes)	Extra point and field goal: punt safe and hang middle

Saturday

Meeting (4:40-4:55 P.M.)	Kickoff cover
Walk-through (6:50-7:00 P.M.)	Kickoff cover: surprise onsides, kickoff with holder
Practice (full)	Mock game

Sunday

Meeting (5:35-5:50 P.M.)	Review mock game
Practice (shells) (7:00 P.M.)	To be announced

Special teams development has to be a total team effort. That effort starts with the head football coach committing the time and players for a successful kicking game. You don't need to have the best overall players on special teams; instead look for the players who can do those tasks the very best. Your best special teams player could be your third-team safety. As long as the coach approaches each phase and each player with the same enthusiasm as he does his offensive and defensive units, the kicking game will show dramatic results.

INDEX

Note: The italicized *f* and *t* following page numbers refer to figures and tables, respectively.

ABOUT THE AFCA

Since its establishment in 1922, the **American Football Coaches Association** has provided a forum for the discussion and study of all matters pertaining to football and coaching. It also works to maintain the highest possible standards in football and the coaching profession. These objectives—first declared by founders Major Charles Daly, Alonzo Stagg, John Heisman, and others—have been instrumental to the AFCA's becoming the effective and highly respected organization it is today.

The AFCA now has more than 10,000 members, including coaches from Canada, Europe, Australia, and Japan. Through annual publications and several newsletters, the association keeps members informed of the most current rule changes and proposals, proper coaching methods, innovations in techniques, insights on coaching philosophy, and business conducted by the board of trustees and AFCA committees. A convention is held each January to give members a special opportunity to exchange ideas and recognize outstanding achievement.

The association promotes safety in the sport and establishes strong ethical and moral codes that govern all aspects of football coaching. In addition, the AFCA is involved in numerous programs that ensure the integrity of the coaching profession and enhance the development of the game. The AFCA works closely with the National Collegiate Athletic Association, the National Association of Collegiate Directors of Athletics, the National Association of Intercollegiate Athletics, the National Football League, the National Football Foundation and Hall of Fame, Pop Warner, and other organizations involved in the game of football. Indeed, one of the goals of the association is to build a strong coalition of football coaches—Team AFCA—who speak out with a unified voice on issues that affect the sport and profession.

The AFCA is the team of the football coaching profession. All current and former football coaches and administrators involved with football are encouraged to join. For more information about becoming a member of the AFCA, please visit the AFCA Web site (www.afca.com) or write to the following address:

American Football Coaches Association
100 Legends Lane
Waco, TX 76706
254-754-9900

ABOUT THE EDITORS

Bill Mallory is Indiana University's winningest football coach, having compiled a 69-77-3 record in his 13-year tenure as head coach. While compiling a 165-121-4 record at Miami (Ohio), Colorado, Northern Illinois, and Indiana, Mallory became one of only a handful of coaches in history to guide three different programs to top 20 finishes in national polls. In 1987, Mallory became the first coach to be awarded back-to-back Big Ten Coach of the Year honors. While at Indiana, Mallory led the Hoosiers to six bowl games, including victories in the 1998 Liberty Bowl and the 1991 Copper Bowl. He also led IU to a top 20 ranking in 1988.

Courtesy of Paul B. Riley, Indiana University Athletics

Don Nehlen, the winningest football coach in West Virginia University's history, served as the Mountaineers' head coach from 1980 to 2000 and posted a 149-93-4 record. Nehlen's career record of 202-138-8 (including nine seasons as head coach at Bowling Green from 1968 to 1976) made him one of only 17 coaches in NCAA history to record 200 wins. Taking WVU to 13 bowl games and 17 winning seasons, Nehlen coached 15 first team All-Americans, 82 all-conference players, six first team Academic All-Americans, and 80 players who went on to professional football. He received Coach of the Year honors from numerous groups and was the unanimous choice as the 1993 Big East Coach of the Year. A member of the Mid-American Conference, Bowling Green, and Gator Bowl halls of fame, Nehlen has a bachelor's degree from Bowling Green and a master's degree from Kent State. A native of Canton, Ohio, Nehlen and his wife, Merry Ann, have two children and five grandchildren.

Courtesy of Don Nehlen

ABOUT THE CONTRIBUTORS

Ron Bernard Aiken has been defensive line coach at the University of Iowa since 1999. In 2002 he was named the American Football Coaches Association (AFCA) Division I Assistant Coach of the Year. Iowa's rushing defense has ranked second in the Big Ten in each of the past three years. Early in his career, Aiken also gained experience in coaching the offensive line and serving as a special teams coordinator. While playing guard and center at North Carolina A&T, Aiken earned all-conference honors. He has a bachelor's degree in history and a master's degree in secondary education from the Citadel.

Courtesy of Sports Information, University of Iowa

Joe DeForest has been the special teams coordinator and cornerbacks coach at Oklahoma State University since 2001. Under his watch, OSU's national rankings rose from 73rd to 10th in net punting, from 67th to 12th in punt returns, and from 92nd to 3rd in kickoff returns. A 13-year coaching veteran, DeForest spent seven seasons at Duke where he was special teams coordinator and outside linebackers coach. The Blue Devils finished the 2000 campaign as the 6th-best team in the nation in net punting and 15th-best team in kickoff returns. Before his coaching career, DeForest played two seasons of professional football in the Canadian Football League.

Courtesy of Oklahoma State University

Courtesy of Sports Information, University of Iowa

Lester Erb has been a wide receiver and special teams coach at the University of Iowa since 2000. Under his tutelage, the Hawkeyes' special teams have ranked among the best in the nation: second in the Big Ten in kickoff returns and third in punt returns in 2003; they have also set a school record with five blocked punts. After gaining experience on the Syracuse and Hobart College football staffs, Erb spent two seasons as the offensive quality control coach for the NFL's Baltimore Ravens and was tight ends coach on the Army staff. Erb was a standout receiver at Bucknell University, where he earned his bachelor's degree in business administration. He also holds a master's degree in higher education administration from Syracuse.

Courtesy of Virginia Tech

Bud Foster is one of the nation's most respected defensive coaches, helping build Virginia Tech into one of the hardest-hitting defensive units in college football. Having coached at Tech since 1987, Foster has helped mold nationally ranked defenses on a yearly basis. His success made him a two-time finalist for the coveted Broyles Award, presented annually to the nation's top assistant football coach. He was also recognized as the 2000 Division I-A Defensive Coordinator of the Year by *American Football Coach* magazine. During his tenure, Foster has coached two All-Americans and six others who have earned All-Big East Conference honors.

Courtesy of John Harbaugh

John Harbaugh is the special teams coordinator for the Philadelphia Eagles. His units finished the 2003 season ranked first in the NFL in the articulate special teams ranking system by the *Dallas Morning News*. In 2001, Harbaugh's peers voted him as the league's Special Teams Coach of the Year. Harbaugh began his coaching career in 1984 at Western Michigan, spent eight seasons as assistant coach at the University of Cincinnati (1989 to 1996), and joined the Indiana University staff as defensive backs and special teams coach in the 1997 season.

Lieutenant Colonel Jeff Hays has coached three All-Western Athletic Conference Mountain division kickers and all-time school leaders in nearly every kicking category. A graduate of the USAF Academy, he has a master's degree in biology and kinesiology from the University of Texas and has also worked as a biology professor and aerospace physiologist through assignments in the United States Air Force.

Courtesy of Jeff Hays

Steve Kidd is the assistant coach and recruiting coordinator for Rice University in Houston, Texas. Kidd has developed a succession of quality performers on special teams, some of whom have gone on to the NFL draft; earned all-WAC honors; and established new school records in kicking, punting, field goal percentages, and extra points. Kidd ended his own collegiate career at Rice with records in career punting average and the highest game average, as well as the best average for a season. In 1993, Kidd was inducted into the Rice Athletic Hall of Fame.

© Bill Baptist/Rice University

Bill Legg was named the offensive line coach at Purdue University in March 2003. He came to the Boilermakers from Marshall, where he served as tight ends coach and recruiting coordinator (2001 to 2002). In both years the Thundering Herd ranked third in the nation in total offense, compiling a 21-4 record and winning two bowl games. Previously, Legg was the interior offensive line coach at his alma mater, West Virginia, where he enjoyed a successful playing career as a four-year starting center and participated in four consecutive bowl games. Legg holds a bachelor's degree in psychology and a master's degree in education.

Courtesy of Bill Legg

Courtesy of Ball State University

Bill Lynch is the head football coach at DePauw University and holds a career record of 73-65-3 over 13 seasons. He served as the head coach of Ball State's football program from 1995 to 2002, during which time his teams won the 1996 Mid-American Conference title, participated in the Las Vegas Bowl, and finished as co-champions of the MAC West Division in 2001. Lynch was head coach at Butler, his alma mater, for five seasons, where his teams compiled a 36-12-3 record. He was named the Heartland Collegiate Conference Coach of the Year three times, earned two Regional Coach of the Year honors from the AFCA, and directed the 1988 team to the NCAA Division II playoffs.

Courtesy of the University of Illinois

Greg McMahon came to the University of Illinois in 1992 and has coached the Illini special teams and tight ends since 1997. McMahon's kickers have averaged more than 12 field goals per season and have connected on an impressive 188 of 191 extra points (.984). Under McMahon's guidance, Illinois' tight ends have accounted for an average of 20 catches, 200 yards, and 3 touchdowns a year. Before joining the U of I, McMahon spent two seasons coaching offensive tackles and tight ends at the University of Nevada at Las Vegas. He also spent time at Valdosta State, Southern Illinois, North Alabama, and Minnesota. McMahon earned his bachelor's degree in psychology from Eastern Illinois University in 1983 after playing four seasons as a defensive back for the Panthers.

Courtesy of the University of Utah

Urban Meyer is the only coach in Utah's 110-year football history to win a conference championship in his first year. In 2003, *The Sporting News* named Meyer National Coach of the Year after he led the Utes to a 10-2 record, their first outright conference championship since 1957, a bowl victory, and a final national ranking of 21. Meyer's special teams led the nation in kick return average and ranked second in the league in kickoff coverage. Meyer began his head coaching career at Bowling Green in 2001, where he engineered the biggest turnaround in NCAA Division I-A football.

Brian Polian is the University of Central Florida's recruiting coordinator and running backs coach. Before joining the Golden Knights, he served three years at Buffalo as the running backs and special teams coach. He previously coached at Buffalo during the 1998 season when he served as tight ends and assistant offensive line coach. Before joining UB, Polian served as the offensive graduate assistant at Michigan State as the Spartans finished 24th in the nation and played in the Aloha Bowl. Polian also spent two seasons at Baylor University, where his duties included coaching the strongside linebackers and co-coordinating special teams.

Courtesy of the University of Central Florida

Joe Robinson is the special teams coordinator and defensive ends coach at the University of Arizona. He has more than a decade of experience as either a recruiting or special teams coordinator. His 2003 special teams units at Central Florida ranked second in the nation with a 41.9 net punting average. Previously, he helped the Houston Cougars lead Conference USA in net punting and coached special teams at Southern Mississippi, which led the nation in kick returns in 1997.

Courtesy of Joe Robinson

Robin Ross is an assistant coach at the University of Oregon, overseeing the special teams and tight ends unit. In 2003, his teams ranked second in the Pac-10 in punt returns. His 2002 special teams were the only squads in the league to rank in the top 20 nationally in punts, kickoffs, and kickoff returns, while Duck punters led the Pac-10 and ranked 10th nationally in net punting. The 27-year coaching veteran has played a role in special teams in each of his last five coaching stops, including a two-year stint at Western Washington from 1994 to 1995. The Vikings were 17-4 during Ross' two seasons, leading the nation in scoring defense in 1994 and serving as the NAIA's top-ranked team for five weeks in 1995.

Courtesy of the University of Oregon

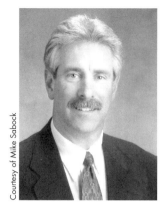

Courtesy of Mike Sabock

Mike Sabock is the defensive ends coach and recruiting coordinator for Northern Illinois University, where he has also served as the Huskies' defensive backs coach and linebackers and special teams coordinator since arriving there in 1984. He was previously an assistant defensive backfield coach at Penn State University under the legendary Joe Paterno in 1983. His Ohio prep coaching stops included Alliance and Youngstown Austin Fitch high schools. Sabock was a two-time All-Ohio Athletics Conference pick at Baldwin-Wallace college, where he earned a bachelor of science degree in health and physical education. He went on to earn a master's degree in athletic administration from Kent State University in 1981.

Courtesy of the University of Alabama

Dave Ungerer, a coaching veteran of 21 college seasons, is a special teams and tight ends coach for the University of Alabama. In 2003, Alabama special teams produced three touchdowns from kick and punt returns (most in the SEC) and five blocked kicks. Ungerer also coached tight ends and special teams at California, finishing 2002 ranked first in kickoff returns and fifth nationally in punt returns. His special teams also accounted for six plays of 50 yards or more that season. Ungerer lettered four years as running back at Southern Connecticut State, where he received his bachelor's degree in physical education and health.

*You'll find
other outstanding
football resources at*

www.HumanKinetics.com

In the U.S. call

1-800-747-4457

Australia.............................. 08 8277 1555
Canada 1-800-465-7301
Europe......................+44 (0) 113 255 5665
New Zealand................... 0064 9 448 1207

HUMAN KINETICS
The Premier Publisher for Sports & Fitness
P.O. Box 5076 • Champaign, IL 61825-5076 USA